No One Deserves A Relationship...

Jameel Watson

Rest in Peace, Grandma

You were my comfort zone. Whenever I was going through something and needed peace, you always provided that. I can finally see the face of the angel that's watching over me...

I love you...

CONTENTS

LOGIC IS WORTH MORE THAN FEELINGS

Whenever I invested feelings into a relationship, I wasn't fortunate enough to get the same energy and effort back in return. I got tired of it. It's draining having to exert energy, while also having to replenish myself once I noticed that my partner was unable to do so.

As I matured, I realized that I went through the same three phases in every relationship. It never failed. When you're in the moment, you don't realize when one begins and when you're exiting one. The more you think your way through relationships, opposed to just feeling your way through one, you'll arrive to the realization as well. The realization that maybe you were never in a relationship to begin with. It amuses me how people think they're in a relationship just because they spend a lot of time with the person they like.

PHAS.E 1: VULNERABILITY

I don't know, maybe I'm just not built for relationships. Things just never seem to work out in my favor. As soon as I get excited about someone, they disappoint me. It happens every time. I'm gradually and unwillingly adjusting to the reality that I'll never find the right individual. It's weird, but it seems as though I do better with spare parts that belong to others, rather than having a whole person to myself. I don't know why that's the case, but I'm tired of that shit. I'm tired of not being able to have my own. I'm tired of not being able to decipher through people who are deserving, and who are just going to waste my time. I'm tired of asking myself why shit never works out. And most importantly, I'm tired of making excuses for people who are making it clear that they don't want to be in my life. And even after realizing all of that, I still try.

Okay, let me be honest; I'm built for relationships, apparently just not the good ones. Either I'm the one causing the toxicity to occur, or it's my person of interest. But there's always an issue. Things can never just go as smoothly as they should. I don't expect things to be perfect, but damn. I shouldn't be experiencing bad situation after bad situation.

And I understand that every relationship has their tribulations; that's not what I'm referring to. I'm referring to issues that cause you to lose your sanity. Issues that cause you to lose sleep damn near every night. Issues that make you question if you're asking too much from your partner. Issues that make you question your worthiness. Issues that lead to you surrendering your peace. Issues that make you question why you're subjecting yourself to mistreatment; but also knowing that you're not leaving the relationship anytime soon. Issues that have you contemplating suicide. That's when you know you're in too deep.

I thank God those suicidal thoughts never got the best of me. Once I put my life at risk in an attempt to get my relationship back, was when I knew that there were issues that were stronger than me. I wasn't aware of how weak I could be. I've been in my room, looking at pills and guessing how many it'll take to either get my woman back, or to kill me. It usually was the same amount for both situations.

I've been in my car contemplating on how my family would deal with this situation if I went through with it. I pictured the speech that would be given at my funeral from the woman I was trying to get back. I wonder what emotions she would display. I'd hope I could get a tear out of her. I'd hope I could get some meaningful story about how good I made her feel, even though that wasn't the common theme in our dealings. I hope she puts on a show in front of my family and friends. No one has to know the truth on how much emotional pain and agony I cost you. Just make me out to be opposite of who I was when we were together. To her, maybe that would be a relief. Maybe she'd appreciate me more as a thought, than her man. I've been there.

I used to think it was a joke when people said you were never in love until you had them kind of thoughts. I remember people telling me that was one of the symptoms that came along with it. That shit is dangerous if it's true. I'm not sure if I want to ever experience love if heartbreak takes me to that place. From my experience, it never went further than thoughts. But I guess that's all that's needed.

And to the woman that I attempted to blame for my suicidal thoughts and acts, I'm sorry. I'm sorry for putting you in a position you didn't ask to be in. I'm sorry for trying to make you culpable for my wrongdoings. No one deserves to have the responsibility of someone else's health on their hands. I was in a dark place. I wasn't secure with myself. I was unable to formulate the conversation that needed to be held in order to prevent this. I just wasn't ready. I'm not saying this excuse my actions, I'm just providing reasoning. I hope you're doing well.

I apologize. This isn't how the book was supposed to begin.

When it comes to relationships, I don't know whether to cherish them, or just get accustomed to dealing with different personalities and then disposing of them once I feel as though I'm satisfied. I've never been one to cherish something that involves another person. It never made sense for me to do so. Sometimes I hate that I'm selfish like that. Even when I notice and give myself the opportunity to change my ways, I disregard my own instincts. Life is always fun when you disregard your better judgment. Most of my memories derives from moments when I disregarded my better judgement. But, I guess this mindset is why I can never find a good relationship. Well, I can find them, I'm just not a fan of them. I'm working on it, though. For some reason, I never give them the opportunity to manifest into something greater than my current vision. I always think the worst is going to happen; mainly because, in all my relationships, the worst has usually happened. And typically, I was the cause of it. I'm bad at this relationship thing. I don't know when to take someone seriously. I don't know when to set aside my own agenda to better serve the interests of my person of interest. I don't know when to ignore the signs that shout to me that the person I'm interested in, is covered in red flags. But it's just something about red flags that grabbed my attention. It's something about them that makes me want to get involved. I'm not sure how I obtained this mindset, but I'm here. There's nothing left to do but to embrace it. So here I am, embracing it.

This doesn't have much to do with anything, but what does it mean when the person you're involved and currently having issues with, leaves for the full night and opts to not answer your calls? No updates on where they are, or even making you aware that they're leaving. That happened to me and it's still bothering me. Bothering me enough to be here talking about it amid my book. I don't want to overreact and make the situation into something it's not, but it just isn't making sense to me. When I woke up in the middle of the night and noticed that she wasn't home, there were a few things that caught my attention. Her charger was missing. Glasses were still there, leading me to believe she put herself in an intimate or comfortable setting. The liquor bottle was also missing. Absence and liquor is just one of those combinations that lead to disturbed thoughts. And I love disturbed thoughts, just not when they're at my own expense.

If I had a friend telling me this encounter as his own, I wouldn't even hesitate with what I think his woman was doing. We all know what's going on. Those aren't common acts. You don't leave silently like that, especially under those conditions. And as a man, it's difficult to show insecurity and question her whereabouts. What man really wants to sit there and show vulnerability in that form? That might be one of our biggest downfalls; openly showing vulnerability. But that's neither here nor there.

And usually I'd agree we shouldn't question their whereabouts; but this isn't one of those situations where I refrained from doing so.

For this woman to tell me that she visited a female friend that I never heard of, nor remember her having recent contact with that person, threw me completely off. Whenever you hear some bullshit in response to a posed question, it just makes you even angrier at the situation and person. Don't play with me like I'm not aware. I don't know if she's as brave as she thinks I'm dumb, or what. But when you care about someone, you at least attempt to absolve them from all possible scenarios that impacts you negatively. Something in me wants to believe that our current situation is leading me to think there's someone else. And there's something in me that wants to believe that our current situation is leading me to overreact and overthink. I guess we make excuses for who we want to make excuses for. It's just hard to ever look at that woman the same again.

We all want our women to reflect us, until they actually start to move in the same manner we do. Nobody wants to put themselves in a position to view their own flaws and behaviors. So, to have a person that embodies exactly what you exude, is scary. But I recognize the sneaky tactics. I've employed those same techniques. I used to leave out late and gently turn the knob to avoid making noise. I used to create alibis with my friends prior to going out so that I can refer to the text messages and call logs to prove my location during times of alleged affairs. I used to make up dumb excuses when I was close to getting caught. I used to make it seem like the person that was confronting me wasn't sure what they were talking about. Most of the time, the person accusing me knew exactly what they were talking about.

But the key is to never say too much. You never know what they're aware of, so don't put yourself in a situation where you're telling on yourself. That's the key; if they allude to knowing certain information, make them prove it.

But I don't know; what do you think? Eventually women get fed up and start to take on the same characteristics that led to them being hurt. I understand the whole having a breaking point idea. I get it. But that's a scary sight; seeing the woman you're involved with turn into the same person that's been hurting her. It's hard to live with that. I hate living with that. I hate knowing that the person I initially met, will never return back to original form. I hope I'm just overreacting. It's damn near two in the morning, and you know how the mind has a mind of its own around these hours. But I feel as though as soon as I put this pen down, I'll condemn her.

But the more I write, the more I forgive her for an act that she's probably not even at fault for. This is why I love writing; I can paint any narrative I want, and the reader has no choice but to feel as though I'm leading them in the right direction. My direction. So, do I stop doing what I love and head to sleep, or do I keep writing to protect the image of the woman I love? I think that's the first time I ever mentioned the word love and this woman together. I'm not sure if I said it because I actually mean it, or if the situation is augmenting my feelings. And I hate that I just questioned that thought in order to protect my own feelings and pride.

Jameel Watson

.   .

Experience vs Longevity

You have to know why you're entering the relationship in the first place. If you're encountering the same issue with failed relationship after failed relationship, step back and try to understand your purpose for being there. What are you ultimately trying to accomplish? I believe there's only two objectives in relationships; experience and longevity. Often times we enter a relationship solely because we like someone and believe that we've established a type of bond that seems undeniable. Whenever a feeling like that surrounds you, you want to embark on that journey, which is understandable. You can't blame anyone for acting on such impulse when that happens. You don't think about the long game. All you know is that you want that person, and all other questions and concerns get handled later. I know that sounds cute and ideal, but that's the same attitude that leads to someone experiencing failed relationship after another. And other times, you just want to be attached to something that has some meaning. At some point in our lives, we all yearn for that. We all want to be included in something that is bigger than ourselves.

How can you debate someone with that goal? It's easy for me, someone you don't know, to tell you what you should value in relationships, right? I'd laugh too if a stranger was telling me what I should and shouldn't expect.

But then again, it's better to trust a stranger who doesn't gain anything from exploiting you, opposed to someone you're familiar with that could.

You don't have to get into a relationship just because you like the person. We have to learn to stop being so quick to react to feelings. We see a face, notice familiarities, get a glimpse of their personality and automatically want to connect ourselves to that person. Then whatever comes from that engagement, is what comes from it. We can't make these decisions on whether we want longevity or experience amid relationship. That's something you have to identify within yourself prior to getting involved. We all know how difficult it is to think clearly when feelings and history get involved. Don't confine yourself to a situation due to the inability to articulate and determine what your wants and desires are. Once you're in a predicament where you're looking for reasons to stay and reasons to leave, the relationship is already ruined. There's nothing worse than your mind leaving the relationship before the body.

And always remember - Do not make questioning your position in someone's life a habit...

.   .

Experience

Sometimes, you just want to try some shit out. You might want to opt to go outside your element and date someone you wouldn't customarily involve yourself with. You'll never know what attracts you and who you could potentially connect with if you aren't vulnerable enough to put yourself in that situation. You have to occasionally step outside your comfort zone for experimental purposes. Trying new things will always attribute to building character. You can't get too comfortable with dealing with your type. You can, but I wouldn't advise it. But who am I? We have a habit of settling. You like what you like, therefore, you entertain what you entertain. But there's more to life than what you like. But I understand; trying new things only seem fun when there's no repercussions. You can't be disappointed if you only entertain what you've been accepting.

Having a type is funny. Ask someone you know what their type is and watch them give you a detailed list. That list, more often than not, will include their height, smile, education, occupation, along with their skin tone, certain personality traits, and a bunch of other bullshit that doesn't mean much in the grand scheme of things. After they provide that list, ask them how many times they have had that type, and just wait. More than likely they'll tell you that they never had it. They just envision what they would like and come to the conclusion that that's all they'll entertain. How can you know if something is your type if you never experienced it? You miss out on great people by eliminating them from your prospects, due to focusing on a certain type of build. How can you not appreciate the learning aspect of experiencing new things? How can you be comfortable dealing with the same thing over and over? That's complacency. If I order the same thing from every restaurant, I'd never enjoy restaurants. I'd be going just to go. I guess some people are fine with playing it safe because they're able to better predict the outcome. I could never subject myself to that.

And who's to say that your type is interested in you? It isn't a sure thing that once you find the person you're looking for, that they're also looking for you. That's the worst; when you like someone who doesn't notice or care to put themselves in a position to like you back. And once you encounter this situation, you're now in the same position as the people you've denied in the quest of finding your type. It's a vicious cycle isn't it? Just be careful with how you treat people in the attempt to find what you're looking for.

Relationships taught me to not treat people how they treat you. I don't know why I ever decided to live by that adage. From now on, I'm treating people how I want to treat them. People love bringing fake energy around, hoping you'll treat them better than how they feel about you. Moving forward, I refuse to subject myself to anyone's alternative motives...

Often times when I entered relationships that I knew wouldn't last long, it was because I wanted to delve into a different type of personality. And in doing so, I lowered the risk of getting hurt, due to having little to no expectations. I loved being in environments where little to no expectations were placed upon me. Sometimes I get tired of producing. I want to interact freely and be myself. I don't always want to be held to a standard that's been socially and or morally constructed. I just wanted to be in a situation where I didn't have to worry about being vulnerable. I wanted to see how my personality changed when the only goal was having fun and not seeking long term commitment. I wanted to embark on that journey. Certain personalities can unlock parts of your character you didn't know you possessed. I was infatuated with learning the new ways I could tell jokes due to a certain person. I was infatuated with gaining a new vernacular due to a certain person. I was infatuated with accumulating new habits due to a certain person. To get a better understanding of yourself, you have to exploit someone else. Well, explore someone else. They're the same if we're being honest.

I loved exploiting other people for my own benefit. Pretending to act or feel a way so you can manipulate them to act and feel a way is a great skill. It took some time to master it, but once I did, I abused it. I abused my ability. I abused their vulnerability. I abused the faith they had in me. I abused their want to help a man that only offered false potential. If you're reading this, I'm sorry. And if I had the chance to do it all over again, honestly, I'd do it again. I'd do it better this time. I'd make my lies more believable this time. I'd make it harder to trust this time. I'm sorry, but I can't allow myself to be as vulnerable as I made you. It doesn't matter how many times I ask for you to take me back; don't. I hope you understand...

When you're focused on achieving a certain task, you tend to unintentionally look over other things of value. I was tired of looking over things that I wasn't aware that I needed.

Looking back, maybe I should've informed the women I used for experience that longevity wasn't my objective. Maybe that would've protected them more. They deserved at least that much. They didn't sign up for that. Every time I look at a woman in my family, I think back and ponder on how men could potentially treat them in the same manner I treated women I dealt with. I definitely should've protected them more. I'm not comfortable with that feeling. I should've shown more appreciation for them. I shouldn't have treated them as if they were disposable; even if they were. I wasn't supposed to let that be known. To let it be known, is to show that I cared. It would mean that I valued the future. I wasn't there for the future. I was there for the experience. If I would have notified them that everything was for experimental purposes, my experiences wouldn't have been genuine. I would've received the reserved version of them. I don't care for that version. Even though I wasn't giving them what they deserved, I wasn't a fan of receiving their reserved side since they would have altered their personality and behavior. I didn't want to receive anything they offered if I didn't request it.

I hate how that sounded. I love the person I was when this was applicable. I hate that I ended up here. I hate that I ended it like that.

Back to the point. Every day, people involve themselves with someone knowing it's going to fail. Which is perfectly fine, as long as you walked into the situation knowing that. For better results and understanding of experience-based relationships, don't tell the person you're getting involved with what you're doing. It isn't worth it. If you can get away with something, get away with it. Because after all, the only way to know if you can get away with something, is if you try to. You worry about the repercussions whenever they arrive; if they arrive. In the meantime, have your fun. I really hate sounding like this, but you'll never fully understand until you've done it. There are people out there that indulge in this same act. There has to be. To appreciate it, is to endure it. I'm sorry if you can't relate. Just understand that there doesn't have to be an end goal attached to every relationship.

Why does it seem like the experienced based relationships are the ones where you have the most fun? It's almost as if the memories that derived from these types of relationships are the ones we cherish the most. Is it the thrill that causes this to happen? I love thrills. I feel like you can be yourself in experienced based relationships. Have you ever had sex with someone you didn't have feelings invested into? How was it?

And when I refer to feelings, I'm talking about deep care, and all that good shit. I'm not referring to having sex with just anyone. From my experiences, that was usually the best sex I've had. I could be myself. Without feelings being involved, I didn't have to worry about how the other person would judge me because they're opinion didn't matter enough to have an impact on me. And when you're just acting without thinking, you enjoy yourself more. You enjoy the moment more because it's not to be thought of later. I feel like there were better examples to prove my point that didn't have to involve sex. I could've exercised my mind more. I hate creating content that revolves around that. When you've been writing all day, sometimes you find ways to create shortcuts that get your point across in a quicker fashion. I want to apologize for it, but this is one of those times where I really don't care.

Since we're here; how do you feel about having sex prior to making someone your boyfriend or girlfriend? That's another thing I'm cautious about in the beginning of relationships. I never know which move to take. Of course, you want to get to know the person before you decide to give your body up to them. We want to feel as though we know the person we're being intimate with. But what if you become fond of the person, but you weren't pleased sexually? What if that's the only issue? I don't know how I'd feel about that. Prior to having sex, if I envisioned a future with you, would I be selfish to ruin what could lead to longevity, due to leaving the relationship because that one area wasn't being fulfilled? How shallow would that make me? Longevity turns into experience as soon as you're not receiving a portion of what's needed. That portion could be the smallest portion, but as long as it's missing, we'll be hesitant to commit.

I've had friends of mine who value longevity speak on how experienced type relationships aren't the most ideal because you'll get used to moving on. They believe that everyone ultimately wants to be in a position of stability. It makes sense. That's the only thing I might hesitate with when deciding how I want to enter relationships. Of course, you have your fun when you're just living life without having any obligations to anyone. Everyone isn't built to carry out obligations that involve more than just themselves. But, so what? What's wrong with constantly moving on? Moving on puts you in a position not to settle.

I don't care what's going on in my life, settling is something I'll never sign up for. So, until I'm comfortable enough with someone to cease this type of lifestyle, I'll be enjoying and experiencing as many people as I want.

Jameel Watson

.   .

Longevity

The ultimate goal of every relationship. For the most part, people want to align themselves with someone who enjoys the destination more than the journey. Wasting time just for the sake of wasting time doesn't sit well with people who aim for permanency. Yes, having the unpredictable lifestyle and temporary thrill is fun and all, but some people want to wake up to the same face every morning; knowing that they have each other's back through everything. There's nothing like being able to see the same face every day and knowing that you both are there because you both share the same aspirations. It's kind of dope when you think about it; knowing that arguments and disagreements won't separate the two of you. When you involve yourself with someone for the experience, once it's over, the relationship is over. That's what you signed up for. It's easy to fall in love and be attached to the experiences people show you, rather than the person themselves. Does that ever happen to you? Enjoying things someone exposed to you, more than the person?

I can imagine that being an uncomfortable position to be in once you come to that realization. Just envision attaching yourself to an individual for the sole purpose of what they can do for you, rather than the person they are outside of the experiences they provide. I guess it's easy to imagine since most of us do it. Actually, we all do it. We all separate the experience from the provider.
It just happens; especially if you're not there for longevity.
Or maybe that doesn't happen with everyone.

I hate projecting my pessimistic ways upon other people. I'm more comfortable with myself if I can make myself believe that I'm not the only one who espouses this mindset. I have to understand that everyone isn't a user like me. Everyone doesn't have ill intent like me. That has to be boring; treating everyone in an honest manner. No one is that genuine. I guess there are people out there who pride themselves on being that. But question; to pride yourself on being genuine, doesn't that make you disingenuous? If I pride myself on being or doing something, to some extent, I'm going out of my way to do it. I'm attempting to do it. Therefore, that would make me disingenuous because I'm attempting, instead of just doing. I don't know… this could just be me trying to justify my behavior. I really don't like the image I paint of myself whenever I write. It's bothersome.

So, it's Father's Day. I always feel a way whenever this day comes around. Seeing how people recall memories, post videos and pictures of their father puts me in a weird space. I can't recall one memory my father and I experienced. Not one laugh. Not one argument. Not one basketball game. Not one teaching and learning moment. Nothing. It's weird because he always knew where I was located, according to some of my older family members. He always had an opportunity to make himself present. Who can just leave their child like that? Who has that mindset to help create something, and then leave it before it can manifest? That's why I feel disgusted when I hear about fathers who attempt to be in their child's life, but their child refuses to entertain or forgive them for whatever wrong they might have done. He's trying, why not allow him to make up for his absence and mistakes? You're that prideful? You're that stuck in your ways that rehabilitation has no room to be proven? And I understand that maybe there's some things that can't be forgiven, which is the reason why the child isn't receptive of their reaching out. I get it. But still, he's trying. I would've gave everything to be able to have a relationship with that man.

Yes, my mother was strong enough to fill the void of his absence; so? In no way should he be absolved, even if I ultimately turned out better due to him not being there. Because who actually knows if I'm a better product now than if he chose to make himself available? No one knows. I have to lie to myself daily about being a better and stronger individual due to his absence. I hate not knowing.

He didn't provide experience or longevity. How crazy is that? But for his other children, he's active and aware. That shit hurt. It hurts knowing he's a father to his other kids, while I'm in my own world making up excuses as to why he's not around.

I really hate this so-called holiday. I hate the aura it brings. I hate the memories I don't have. But, I thank you. For what, I don't really have the answers to. Aside from my amazing mother, I got myself here. I taught myself how to be a man. The things you did, are the exact things I'll never do if I'm fortunate enough to have children of my own. I don't even know if I'm talking to you or the readers. I hope this is you reading this. I really do. Thank you.

I don't have a good track record with relationships lasting longer than the experience stage. I never stay long enough. I guess him and I are more alike than I hoped. I go from experience to experience. Person to person; looking to fill this void that doesn't exist. Maybe I'm not okay with being alone. I've been alone for so long, that I'm starting to view it as some type of dysfunction. Maybe that's been what's bothering me while writing this book. I hate battling demons publicly. Dealing with them alone puts me at peace. A weird kind of peace. I can't really explain it. All I know is that I'm not comfortable with shedding light on my own issues. Then again, who is? Who's that comfortable? It's easy to disguise my issues by placing them on others. That's always fun. That enables me to be aware of my faults, by making the person I'm dealing with responsible for having the same issues. Why should I be the only who has to deal with my faults? That doesn't make sense to me.

Honestly, I have no idea what longevity even looks like, so I'm not even sure if I'm qualified to speak on this subject. The only stable figure in my life has been my mother. Anything other than that, either came and went, or was never present to begin with. And sometimes, you have to just accept everything that comes and goes, as well as the things you've never had.

Everything isn't meant to be experienced. Sometimes it's what you don't experience that builds your character. People always allude to character being identified and created by the things you've endured. But from my perspective, it was the opposite.

I'm not someone who advocates for their environment dictating their behavior and thinking process. I can't imagine being weak enough to blame certain acts based on environment. Maybe weak is the wrong word. Or maybe it's just fitting. We have to learn how to say what we want to say, instead of trying to use euphemisms when speaking to an audience. But I believe we are all stronger than our environment and experiences. It's what we haven't endured that responsible for who we are.

I manage money a certain way due to never being in a position to be careless with it. Therefore, I have to be cautious and aware of how I handle it. I can't afford to be irresponsible. The fact that I'm unable to irresponsible leads me to make different decisions. Once you continue to consistently make decisions due to living and behaving a certain way because of what you lack, it naturally becomes part of your character. That plays a more vital part in your molding, than what you're experienced. Over time, once you keep living the same lesson, it becomes embedded in you. It becomes, you. You are your habits, not what you experience. This behavior all derives from me never being in a wealthy position. You're always going to have people that are willing to combat these types of philosophies. That's the best part; having to back up everything you say. And if you're one of those people that feel the opposing way about this, get to the end of this piece and we'll talk about it.

But the more I ponder on it, I question why I never experienced a long-lasting relationship. Why does it always seem to end quicker than the ones my family and friends are involved in? I don't know; maybe I embrace going from person to person because I'm unwilling to take accountability for my lack of effort and honesty in my dealings. Maybe longevity doesn't exist. In some instances, I expect more from my partner. And in other cases, I find myself coming up short when it's time to reciprocate the love my partners were willing to give me. Seems as though I can never find that balance. I doubt that I ever will. I don't understand why this is so difficult. I understand that I'm the cause of the tribulations I face, but that shouldn't keep me from finding longevity; even though I'd most likely dispose of it if I ever encountered it.

Is it just me? Reading over what I write really bothers me. Apparently, everything does. I hope I'm not alone when I talk to you. If you can't relate, there has to be somebody that does, right? Do you ever have these conversations with yourself? You want to justify and minimize all your wrongdoings, while at the same time hoping people understand your point of view so that you aren't judged if you're unable to probably justify your wrongdoings. Sometimes you just want people to understand you without having to explain. That's one of the best feelings; being understood. That quiet understanding goes a long way. That's what we all want.

I feel as though I did the previous passages a disservice. Not being in a position to speak on something I wasn't fortunate enough to endure aggravates me. Why is it that I'm unable to find the right one? I mean, clearly, I know I'm the reason, but still. Why can't someone cross my path and make me want to change? Although I like being right as it pertains to my relationship ideologies, I'd love to get proven wrong by someone. I'd love for someone to cross my path and debunk everything I've experienced and show me something different in life. Show me that there's more to capture than what I've been exposed to. Show me that a damaged individual can be rehabilitated. Show me that I've been settling, and that longevity can be obtained. Just show me something different. That's all.

Truth is, I wish I had someone to do everything with. Wish I could just get a glimpse of that. I feel like the absence of my father and ex-girlfriend is what causes me to feel like that. Every curiosity and questions that I have, they seem to be a part of the answer. The two people I have no communication with, are the ones who I rely on most for answers. Life is funny like that. But in a way I understand. The people you'd do the most for, are not the people who you have the most communication with. I'm not sure why we're designed like that, but it is what it is.

If we're being honest, we're always going to make the decisions we want to make prior to entering relationships. There's no amount of advice that can and will deter us from doing so. We see all the signs. We know what's beneficial and detrimental to us. We know the risks that are being taken when we choose to take a particular course of action. Sometimes, we just want to see how shit goes. We want to see if we can be the one to change routine behavior. I used to feel a way when I realized the person I liked didn't need any alterations. I didn't want anyone "premade". I wanted to play a part in architecting. I wanted to be the one that's responsible for the maturation process for someone. To be able to do so is an accomplishment. Whenever you're the reasoning for something improving, you value it more. You show it off more. So, it makes sense as to why some people might stay in certain situations with people when things aren't going as well as they would like.

Personally, I would rather entertain people that I know could be the best for me, even if the beginning stages are filled with bullshit and disappointments. I'm not really sure how I define best, but I just know. Whoever can give me the most happiness? I don't know.

Funny how fast I just changed my answer.
Basically, I loved turning the wrong person into the right one. Purposely picking the wrong person was fun for me. I actually got addicted to doing so. There's nothing like having fun with the wrong person. Knowing that things might not work, but just hoping in some way that it all works out is always a thrill. Collaborative toxicity plus physical attraction is a great experience.

I don't know… maybe I'm just a better author than a partner. Seems as though I can express my feelings more willingly in a book, than I can to my partner. I look forward to writing. I'm hesitant to speak on how I feel in my dealings. This just isn't for me. I'm fine being alone. I don't need to experience anyone or accrue longevity to fulfill my purpose in life. I'm more of an idea and message, opposed to a love interest. And I'm comfortable here.

<u>NOTES</u>

<u>NOTES</u>

PHASE 2: PRESERVE THE BATTERIES

I used to hate opening up the freezer and seeing batteries sitting on the door handle. I was one of those kids that used anything around me as a toy, so batteries in plain sight probably wasn't one of the best places to put them. I used batteries as action figures; moving them like they were penguins. I don't know why I chose that movement, but there really isn't another way to give batteries mobility. My friends and I used to throw them in open fields, just to see who was the strongest out of the bunch. And at our worst, we used them as weapons against each other whenever we got bored. But we never thought about putting them in the freezer. Didn't really see the purpose. You never lick the side of a battery when you were a kid? Never wondered what it tasted like? You never cared enough to find out, right? I couldn't have been the only child who had experienced this. For some strange reason, I recall taking a battery out the freezer and placing my tongue on the metal side of it. I can't exactly recall the taste, but I almost tricked myself into thinking I should recreate the scene, just so I can explain it better. I almost did it. I don't know what caused me to lick the batteries, but as a kid, you don't really need a reason to do anything.

I wonder why my mom didn't just throw them out or send me to the store to get some new ones. Any other time she didn't have an issue with sending me on store runs. I always asked myself that question. But I guess as a parent, you don't really need to explain anything to your child. It seemed as though whenever I walked into the kitchen and was tempted to dispose of the batteries in the freezer, she'd be right there, giving me a look that said, "you better not." For some reason, those stare-downs happened a little too frequently; as if God was tired of her doing the same thing and wanted to present me the opportunity to step up and announce my dismay. Of course, I was never that brave and stupid enough to do such a thing. I don't know what household you grew up in, but doing things like challenging your mothers' philosophies, or even making eye contact with her too long was seen as a form of disrespect. I wonder how that would've turned out; stepping up to her. You ever play a full scene in your head about what would ever happen if you chose to do something dumb like that? And the funniest part is, it doesn't matter how many scenarios you play in your head, you lose every time. As soon as you think you have her, she does some mom shit and gets the best of you. I hated not being able to imaginarily outsmart that woman.

Have you ever reached your breaking point? Telling all your friends that you're running away? And what did that one good friend always tell you?

"You can stay with me; my mom won't care."

Something along those lines. Knowing damn well they didn't have the authority to make that decision. But at that moment, that's all you needed to hear to provide some sort of comfort. I remember I planned a full runaway escape in my room. I was having whole conversations with myself; crying, snot all in my nose trying to figure out what to pack. I always packed that one toy and my favorite shirt. You know that one shirt. Whether it's clean or dirty, you're still putting it on. What were some of the things you packed with you? And don't act like you were never in this situation. We've all been there. I'm always intrigued to see how different people react to similar situations. Have ever thought about the new friends you'd have to make? The new lifestyle you'd have to adopt? I don't know why we took life so serious as a kid. Did you ever tell a story that has no purpose, but chose to say it anyway, just because you have an audience?

"Don't touch those batteries. They're not dead, they just need a break."

Mothers are filled with aphorisms. I always laughed to myself whenever she said that. I know my mother wasn't the only one who used the battery in the freezer technique. You never wondered how that worked? Never wondered how the batteries were just able to gain new life? It was always weird to me how a low battery can be restored by simply preserving and shelving it. That dynamic is something I don't think I'll ever stop questioning. But the more I think about it, the more it makes sense, that I shouldn't make sense of it.

Maybe that's one of the keys to relationships; to be content with leaving things unanswered. Knowing what you don't know is beneficial at times. You prevent yourself from being in situations that could potentially embarrass or expose you. It takes an intelligent person to be aware of knowing what they don't know. And if I'm being honest, I have never witnessed or experienced a relationship ending due to curiosity or unanswered questions.

It's always the confirmation that leads to departure. It doesn't matter how skeptical, or how many questions you have regarding your partner's suspicious actions, you always stick around until you know for sure. Nothing is wrong with this process; it's just human nature to get to the bottom of things before making a decision. Even if you have enough evidence to back up your assumptions, you never make that final decision until you catch them. You can't let all the investigative work you've done go to waste by making a judgment solely off curiosity; you did it to be completely certain.

I'm an advocate for believing curiosity is what keeps relationships entertaining and stable. Once the unknown becomes known, there's less to hold onto. I need something to hold. I need to have something to fumble. Not saying that I look forward to fumbling it, but I need something to keep me engaged and on my toes. I don't need the answers, I just need to know there are answers. It seems like a peculiar philosophy to subscribe to, but maybe this is an ideology that needs to be espoused. You don't reach longevity with predictability and plain engagement. Although, I am aware that there are couples out there that experience mundane acts in the relationship. It's just scary because you run the risk of becoming accustomed to it. You involve yourself in that type of relationship for so long, your relationship goes into auto pilot mode; just going through the phases, not really feeling anything. I can't imagine living a life of dullness, just so that I can involve myself with security. What do you look forward to daily in those situations? Where does the excitement derive from? What makes you wake up and feel eager to spend the day with your partner? I understand the greater good, for lack of a better phrase, is what some people seek to find, but this route isn't one I can side with. I can't live like that. I'd rather involve myself with multiple unsuccessful relationships, if it meant that I felt alive throughout its course. If I'm being honest, the shorter my relationships have been, the happier I was.

But why do people feel as though they need to know everything? What does that do? What satisfaction do you get? I guess it varies from person to person. The funny thing is, when you do end up finding out all the details about something, you don't do anything about it. People just love to be nosy. They keep the information stored away until they find a purpose for it. Have you ever had some information on someone you didn't particularly like, so you did petty things and made slick comments to get them to retort, so you could have a reason to expose what you know? But it always seems like as soon as you get ready to play your hand, they get real submissive and calm, as if they've realized your purpose for the confrontation. I wish I could be that ruthless. Even though I don't have that type of behavior in me, I still want to have the information. Who cares if I never use it. But I guess for some, being in a position to prove knowledge, is more convenient than being ignorant.

What's the point of debating about the batteries being in the freezer and me heading to the store to replace them, if the end results both lead to the remote working again? My mother's response to a problem was to try and preserve the batteries by putting them away. I get it. Clearly, she believes that's the remedy to redeeming and restoring. I guess I shouldn't question her method if that works for her. Shouldn't that be the only thing that matters; a solution to a problem, not how you arrived to it?

If your woman says something you don't necessarily understand or agree with, so what? Don't question it. I learned that it doesn't matter what you say, her mind isn't changing. Whatever you say in response to her statement, is just the beginning of a new argument that you won't win. Learning how to take losses in order to keep a happy home is the formula. And if you actually pay enough attention to what they're proposing, it's more logical than you'd think. They just be knowing what's best for you. They're like a substitute mother. They know which friends of yours are not helping you become a better person. They know the foods you shouldn't consume because they're bad for your health. They know which females like you based off the interactions they have with you. They're aware of what business ventures you should embark on, and the ones stay away from. I always wanted to know where they got that skill from. If it was instinctual or taught. Or maybe they're so good with exuding conviction, that we just take heed to whatever they're proposing. Either way, don't question it.

If your man does something that's unconventional or impulsive, don't question it. I don't know why don't take heed to our advice as much as they want us to listen to theirs. We see things before they happen; trust me. And I'll just leave it at that. I'm not about to make this one of those lectures. If your mother says leave the batteries in the freezer, leave the batteries in the freezer. Mothers never steer you wrong.

"They're not dead, they just need a break."

For some reason, that saying keeps popping up in my head. Do you agree that sometimes a relationship can be restored by giving it a break? What are the benefits of giving a relationship a break? And before we get into that, what does a break even mean? We all have our definitions of what constitutes a break. And more often than not, we use it as a way to conceal behavior that we know our partner would condemn us for. It does seem more logical to employ that strategy, than to go out and cheat on your partner. I always thought whoever brought up the idea that going on a break was beneficial for the relationship, was using that excuse as a tool to do what they really wanted to do. Am I wrong for believing that a break implies that there has been a progression in one of your partner's candidates? At least that's how I moved. Why else would you want prematurely depart from your partner?

I remember when I was a candidate. I had all the privileges her boyfriend had, minus the attitude. I never had to deal with that. That was only a problem her man had to handle. I always wanted to thank him for that. He allowed for her and I's engagement to be more entertaining and stress free. If you're reading this, thank you. I'm sure you know who you are. You made my job much easier, and the benefits I received that much greater. I hope you find the one someday.

But I was living the life. I was getting rewarded with meals, back rubs, intimacy, and the jokes her man didn't appreciate. I didn't really enjoy the jokes that much either, but everything is funny when you're getting rewarded for just being there. I wasn't stupid enough to interrupt what she was providing. It was almost as if she was trying to prove to herself that she's a great woman by catering to me to the fullest extent, while also sneaking around on her man. It gave me that "see what he's missing out on?" feeling. Sounds stupid, right? But who was I to disrupt her? I got what I wanted, while making her feel wanted by being present. Most of her dialogue was centered around not being happy in her relationship, and her needing a break so she could, "find herself". To this day, I still don't know what women mean when they say that. I just assume it implies that they want to have fun without having to explain themselves to someone. Something like that. I get it. While she was telling me that she needed a break, I was thinking to myself that I am the break she was referring to. That's when I learned that breaks are people, not a timeframe. It was repeated too often from her, for me to not pick up on it. I'm pretty sure she knew that as well. Some things just work out better when it's not discussed but understood. We knew what we were doing.

Thinking back, I hate that I took advantage of her like that; especially because I never had plans on making her my woman even if her relationship ended. I used to play mind games with her, making it seem as though she could rely on me. I had her believing that I could ultimately be her emotional and security blanket. I was good at it, too. Good to the point that I was almost convincing myself that I meant everything I was saying. I used to mention how I offered emotional security due to being overprotective of my mother. Women love hearing that type of shit. They assume because you take care of your mother, they'd receive the same treatment. I don't know why they arrived to that conclusion. I hinted that I wouldn't put them in the same situations that men prior to me put them in. I was saying everything with so much conviction that I started surprising myself. Whenever I sensed that she was believing the bullshit I was spewing, I'd go distant for a day or two, and dialed back on talking to her. I couldn't afford for her to get comfortable enough to invest in a product that was falsely advertised. If you're reading this, I'm sorry.

Realistically, don't we all have candidates? People who are willing to be there for you, even if you don't see a future with them? Let us not pretend as if we are too good of a partner to have our curiosity stroked by others. How I internalize it, a break just means that I still fuck with you, but there's other options that are doing enough for me to see what I could gain from them. Don't you hate greedy people? It's a sick feeling knowing that it doesn't matter how happy you make someone; they're still liable to entertain someone who doesn't even offer half of what you do, just for the sake of curiosity.

It bothers me how it doesn't matter what I'm doing, the memory of my ex's always finds a way to make themselves present. If I made you happy, it shouldn't matter what another man can do for you. I'm doing for you. And I don't even care if you're fake happy, I just need something to keep my ego intact. I never cared enough to evaluate if it's genuine or not because that didn't concern me. As long as I felt good, everything was good. I hate making them relevant in situations they don't need to be. I feel as though I'm a walking paradox because instead of saying I wanted to take a break, I just did my own thing while still having the privileges of having a girlfriend. But then again, we've all entertained more than we could handle. I believed that if I could be happy with one woman, imagine how happy I could be with multiple. I'm glad that I got that out of my system; well, allegedly, right?

It's difficult to stand by your partner when they're lacking attributes and abilities that you desire. It doesn't matter how much you care about them, no one wants to feel stuck when there are other people willing to provide what you need. Eventually, you'll feel as though it's necessary to create some space between your partner so that you aren't saturated with their faults. And if we're being honest, sometimes, we all need a break. We all need to escape to a pocket that can help us build tolerance for a situation that's temporarily in turmoil.

It's sad because it doesn't matter how much you enjoy what you've been given from your partner; the sight or mystery of something new is captivating.

Something more interesting to me, are the people who opt to request time away from their partner when the relationship is going well. That has always been funny to me. Do you think it's because they aren't accustomed to being happy and catered to, so they shy away from it? Or is it because they're aware that they are not deserving of the treatment that they are receiving from their partner? I guess those perspectives can align in a way. I just don't understand why someone would choose seclusion, especially when they're receiving everything that they wanted from someone. Or maybe they act this way because they're receiving what they wanted, but from the wrong person. Don't you hate when the wrong person offers everything you want? It doesn't matter how hard you attempt to manipulate your mind to just be happy with the relationship, you know that your heart isn't it in. For the wrong person, people have stayed around for a lot less happiness; solely because they wanted to be there. There's nothing like wanting to be there. It seems like people naturally attach themselves to situations that exude toxicity, because the people that provide that, gives them the most memories and that certain feel. There's nothing like that feel. You know exactly what I'm referring to. It can't be explained, but once it consumes you, you know. I want to leave this alone because I'm beginning to experience flashbacks of someone who doesn't deserve to be thought of at this moment. Sorry.

I'm mad that I find a way to incorporate you in everything that I do. All my writings... all my thoughts... all the women that I encounter. For some reason, you're there. You seem to be more present when you're distant, than next to me. I miss you being next to me. But I appreciate you more now that I'm alone. It's a weird feeling. I feel like there's things we could've worked on if we gave it more time. I'll never forgive time for allowing you to give up on me the way you did. Again, I'm sorry.

I never really sat down and appreciated a woman's skill to be able to find a new candidate so quickly. Why are women so adept at finding someone else to entertain when they depart from the relationship? Even if they don't like the new guy, they have the ability to convey that message. Is this some sort of game women play? Do women enjoy using men as tools to accomplish whatever feat they deem as important or fun? I'm more curious about how they find new candidates in the speed in which they do. Then again, maybe they had them around during the relationship; keeping them hidden until a situation arises and causes for them to unveil their new prospect. I'll never know. I'm all for creating security blankets in the event that certain things don't pan out as expected; but to keep someone in your back pocket and have the heart to openly involve yourself with someone else after the separation, is wild to me. But, it's also wild how I'm sitting here pretending as though men don't do the same thing. It's just different when you're not the person of interest anymore. I don't know; I'm starting to depreciate this process the more I think about it. Women are some talented creatures. When I think about how fast they're able to replace you, it makes me think that they purposely bait you into departure. They do and say certain shit that they know will get a reaction from you. Some women get off on being able to accomplish this. The arguing becomes more frequent. Things that never bothered them in the past, all of sudden annoys them. Their will to understand dissipates. They start to listen in order to respond, instead of listening. Your jokes don't seem to be as funny as they once were. They aren't concerned if you ate or not. They make dinner without setting aside a plate for you. They sleep a little closer to their side of the bed. We all know how women love to sleep on their man's side of the bed. Have you ever notice these things? It's disheartening to watch; especially when it's happening right in front of you.

What's worse; knowing that it's over, or watching everything fall apart? It hurts watching the relationship fall apart. It hurts more when it seems as though trying to save it, is what's making it fall apart quicker. You think back to all the memories you and that person shared. All the laughs the two of you created. All the nasty things you've done to each other. All that, just to be on the verge of separating. That's a strange experience. I don't understand how you get to the point of turning your back on each other after enduring so much with one another. When you look at that person, it's hard for them to resemble the person they were before things worsened. It's a scary sight. Almost frightening, due to you now being hesitant in your decision to be in a relationship with anyone else. Nobody wants to go through that again.

Knowing that it's over can be just as damaging, if not worse for some people. The arguments are done with. There's no more sharing of space. The energy you exerted in the relationships no longer has a home. It's quiet. For some, the same things that caused them headaches, are the same things that lead to them creating memories. Some people actually look forward to those things. They only way to be attached to someone is to go through some shit with them. Those are the rules. I don't know which dilemma to side with. I guess the best option is to never be in that position to begin with.

Would you believe that some women would opt to be left, opposed to leaving on their own? It helps them feel less guilty for the next move they're planning on taking once the departure ensues. Women are calculated. I'm not sure if they do this on their own will, or if it's the power of their friends that egg them on to do so. Either way, they're calculated. As the man, it's a hard thing to notice if you aren't focusing on it. And in the rare occasion that you do notice all of the tactics they're employing to get you to leave, it's because they want you to. They're tired of you not catching on to the hints. They want you to be fully aware of their inevitable level up, which doesn't include you. They're fully aware of what makes a man tick; especially their man. But as the man, once you finally understand what's happening, never react. If a woman wants to leave, there's nothing you can do about it. The only thing you're in control of is whether the process is either expedited or delayed. Just don't react. The more you react, the less calm she becomes. And before every storm, there's a calm.

Have you ever walked into your bedroom after your partner cleaned it? You notice that the bed is made up, the room smells better, the carpet is cleaned, your dresser is organized, the clothes are off of the ground, the blinds are straightened. Due to how clean, spacious, and maintained the room has become, you think to yourself that everything between you and your partner is fine. Because, why wouldn't it be? Why would your partner do such a task if they didn't care about you? That's what you do in relationships; clean up after one another. And if the relationship progressed far enough, then sharing and cleaning a living space is a natural act. For all the men; you don't think that act has some underlined meanings? You don't view that as a sign that something has changed? I guess in that moment, why would you? From a man's perspective, we're taking the act for what it is. The room we share was cluttered so they did what girlfriends typically do. We believe everything is how it's supposed to be, especially if you are a man that subscribes to the philosophy that women should keep every room of the house in order, as long as the man is providing.

Quick question; What's your stance on men and women splitting the bills? Do you believe that due to both parties occupying the space, all of the bills should be divided equally amongst the two? I've had this debate with both sexes, and of course, all the answers varied. There were men believing that since they both share the same space, there should be no difference in pay. To an extent, I understand that stance. But, I believe as a man, if capable, we cover rent, while the women take care of the home. As I explained that to some of the men, one retorted in a way that almost made me change my position. His point was that if he was not present, and the woman lived on her own, she would be responsible for paying for everything on her own. He felt as though there shouldn't be a dispute on going half if the latter means taking care of all the bills by yourself. It's kind of difficult to disagree with sound logic.

On the other hand, you know the women had their own philosophies. Some were so adamant in their stance that men should be the provider and pay for everything; while they save their money and spend it on whatever they feel is important. I don't know, I always thought that having a place to lay your head down was important. Maybe I'm wrong. But the more opinions you hear, eventually some of them will begin to make sense. Some explained to me how men expect gender roles to be carried out by women, as it pertains to a cleaned house, made food and nurturer, but choose not to create a household for those requests to get done. I had no response to that. It's hard to disagree with sound logic.

But back to the room. The less that's shown, the more that's hidden. In the mind of a woman that's fed up, that room is cleaned for a different purpose. Why is it assumed that your woman cleaning is a healthy sign in the relationship? Do men not understand that women clean under all conditions? Whether they're bored, agitated, lonely, or in great spirits, they'll clean if the opportunity arises. To a woman that's fed up, that room is cleaned for a different purpose. We're appreciating the aesthetics and act; she's already beginning the process of devaluing your importance in her life. It's some evil thoughts that go through women's minds when they're mad and cleaning. That a speech you never want to be around for. And the occasional stare-downs and glances while doing so speaks volumes.

You're not even aware that she has her bags packed and just waiting to give her departure speech. Of course, the room is going to look clean once all her belongings are no longer scattered around the room. The better maintained the environment is, the better they can deliver that speech. For some reason, most women deliver the shit out of that speech. They've evolved from the "it's not you, it's me" mantra. They're now telling us that we're not productive. That we're not in a position to aid in their progression. Telling us how they made so many sacrifices to keep the relationship afloat. Assuring us that we won't be able to find another woman that provided as much as them through the course of the relationship.

Whenever men hear that speech of dismay, they start to break. They start stuttering more than they already do. Everything hits at once. But then again, if things didn't work out, why would they want somebody that resembles their ex? Isn't that the purpose; to not deal with someone that has the same character? Isn't that part of the reason why it didn't work? But regardless, witnessing a man break in front of you isn't a pleasing sight. Their whole character changes. The man you initially knew, that was so nonchalant and too cool to care, starts to bring all their emotions out. All of a sudden, they're willing to listen more. They're willing to be understanding, and more level handed. It's kind of funny the transformation they go through after hearing that they're partner has had enough. Men say they want honesty, right? I guess we all do, until we're on the recipient end, rather than being the one who delivers it.

And then you have those suave, sophisticated women who depart in a different fashion. They mention how your aura and energy isn't conducive to their premise in life. They mention how there's a greater purpose for you and her, that doesn't involve the two of you being together. All types of sayings that lead you to actually believe that the breakup is beneficial. You have to stay away from those types of women; they're dangerous with words. The more you ponder it, women are some special beings. To be able to take a room, and have it embody two different meanings depending on how they feel, is a special talent. I can never look at a clean room the same when in the midst of a relationship.

Sometimes, I hate when and how I speak. I work in the mindset that everything is a dependent variable; there's no contingencies. If you perceive someone as toxic, and takes advantage of you, then there's something within you that isn't strong enough to combat that behavior. Even though I don't necessarily subscribe to that, the way I deliver alludes to the fact that I do. I have to be careful with that because it's easy to create a victim blaming narrative with certain words and beliefs. But here I go, acting as if I care. Acting as if I value any opinion that isn't mine or my mother's. I never really cared, but it's fun to pretend to. That's why I'm probably better off being just an author, opposed to a companion. I don't have to burden the responsibility of someone else's feelings. I hate being responsible for other people's feelings. How they feel will never mean more to me than how I feel about myself. Never. But regardless of how nonchalant I am, I try to care. I really do. Nonchalant just means I lack emotion, not feelings. It's hard for me to identify who I really am. You ever have that battle within yourself? When do you arrive to the conclusion of who you are? You never will. That's a journey with no destination. I really hate self-reflecting. Because who am I to argue with the accurate picture of myself that I illustrated? At the same time, I feel some kind of way. I want people to care for me in ways I'll never care about them. But how can I request that due to the unwillingness to reciprocate? Ultimately, I don't know if I'm secure with myself or not. Am I confident, or am I just a voluntary victim? I'll answer that on my own time.

Why do women always tend to look better when the relationship is no longer active? And they always seem to be doing better in life. After every break up, there seems to be this new radiance that comes upon them. I heard women refer to it as a, "no fuck boy" glow. I guess that makes sense; less stress, better life. You don't know if you should feel bad for holding them back or take credit for aiding them to become a better person. I think that's the only way men can cope with the situation. We'll find a way to keep our ego intact. We all want to take credit for something; especially if we no longer are privileged enough to possess it.

Just imagine you picking your woman's outfit; the shirt, pants, shoes, jewelry, perfume, all that. You put your thoughts and finances into it. You took the time out to pay attention to details and accessories, just to see her leave your life in the same ensemble that you constructed. Don't you hate when you depart from someone, and in the back of your mind you know for certain that they're taking everything they've learned from you and using it with the next person? Watching other men compliment her on her wardrobe, while she uses your jokes and lingo to impress them. It's disturbing. That's the type of shit that will make any man sick to his stomach.

Speaking of stomach; is "boyfriend weight" a real thing? The happier women are, the bigger they get? I didn't mean for it to sound that way. I always assumed that women used that for an excuse to justify their true eating habits. You know in a relationship, typically, the man's money is used to feed his woman. Once involved with a man, you never really see women using their own finances to get food. And honestly, that's exactly how it's supposed to be. People are always hungrier when their money isn't being used to purchase or provide food.

Ok, so, is boyfriend weight premeditated weight? What I mean is, is the weight you gained the real you? I'm aware of how different moods alter eating habits, so my belief is that once someone finds a comfort pocket, they unravel to the person they're meant to be. I always thought this only pertained to personalities, but it seems to be pertinent in eating as well. I know when I experienced periods of being broke, my taste buds adjusted to what I could afford. Everything that was cheap somehow found a way to taste good. Whenever I was back on my feet and living comfortably, those same foods I enjoyed while broke, never got my attention again. The real me came back in affect. Do you see where I'm going with this?

Why don't men blossom in the same fashion during a separation? That might've been my first time every saying the word blossom aloud. And then I coupled it with the word fashion? But you never wondered why men seem to fall off a cliff after departure? It's damn near scary seeing that transition. The weight that women lose, it seems as if we find it. I don't know how that happens, but it's kind of creepy. And what is it about the women looking better to us, and us looking less desirable to them? Is there some type of process that initiates that, or is it an immediate capability woman possess? Or could it be that you felt like this the whole time, but you shielded those feelings and flaws because you were so invested in that man? I know most women experienced dealing with a man that didn't necessarily meet their physical standards but entertained him anyway because they felt as though he had potential in other areas. And what do we do as soon as we entertain a woman we know is out of our league? That's right; we start showing our ass. We start to act as if she's the lucky one. And don't get me wrong, there's a lot of quality men out there that deserve to be courted as well. But if we're just being honest about this, most of the time, men are the recipient of the blessing. But can you blame us for feeling like we're the prize when we have a woman we know is out of our league on our side? Shouldn't you want your man to walk around egotistically? You should want him to feel more confident when he speaks and acts, even if you have to deal with some of the arrogance.

Knowing you instilled that confidence doesn't excite you? That doesn't make you feel good in any kind of way? When you're partially responsible for this behavior, you can't penalize him for it. So how can you turn around and dispose of him for the things you implanted? Women are vicious. They're a whole different person when they're not committed to you anymore. How you ever witnessed how fast an "I love you' turns into an "you ain't shit" speech? The same man you laid in bed and shared aspirations with, is now this person who you despise. The more I think and write, I start to appreciate the relationship that I don't have.

Mentally, I'm not stable enough to give myself to another individual without knowing their genuine feelings at all times. I don't have the patience. Do you ever feel as though you just vibrate at a different level than most people in this generation? Feeling as though the effort you exert could never be reciprocated because it could never be understood in this climate of microwave relationships. My shit is not microwavable. My shit cannot be digested quickly. My shit cannot be consumed and forgotten about briefly afterwards. I am not convenience. I am not a vibe; I am substance. What the fuck is a vibe? I hate how people use the word 'vibe' nowadays. Relying on an aura to take the place of communication doesn't sit well with me.

Do you come to your senses while you're on a break from your partner, or do you lose them? Do you realize your worth, or do you start to think you're worthless to that person? For some, the more time you are separated from them, the more the idea forms that maybe you weren't the best person for them. I know that might seem a little dramatic, but you'd be surprised the sunken place people go into. I hate to sound so cheesy and banal, but have you ever dealt with someone who developed a broken heart prior to you? All the bullshit you have to go through just to earn their trust, and for them to believe you won't hurt them. It's annoying and tiring, isn't it? So, imagine how distraught and detached that person is. A break from a relationship is more than a break from a relationship. Did you ever come across someone whose whole life revolved around their partner? Everything that happens to their partner impacts their life as well. It's scary when their partner is all they have. If you're their significant other, how do you deal with knowing you may have to conceal how you really feel? Or that you may have to avoid certain conversations and actions because their whole life is determined by how you maneuver? I would hate that. Imagine not being able to express that you're unhappy and want to move on to something new, but you can't because you're liable to put their mental health and safety at risk. I don't think anyone should have to carry the burden of sheltering a situation that isn't advantageous for them, just to console someone who could solely just be using them as a crutch. Imagine not knowing the real them until the relationship is over.

Just picture being fully consumed with someone day in and day out; having all your mannerisms deriving from them. It gets to the point where you are them. I don't know if that's admirable or alarming; you can decide that.

But imagine being consumed with someone, then all of a sudden that comfort net disappears. Do you know how frightening that is? Having a reliable structure suddenly vanish could cause anyone agony. Even though I believe that everyone should be a product of relationship agony, I would hate for it to become pertinent due to scenarios like these. When instances such as a security net departs from you, it could cause for anyone to regress to a state of vulnerability and permanent seclusion. Your psyche takes an everlasting hit, but depending upon how you rehabilitate, there's a possibility for recovery. There are people who I've encountered who refutes this idea. They don't believe situations similar to ones I described impedes as much as I claim it does. They live by the motto that life goes on, so they don't believe that someone's dismissal aids in them being mentally disturbed or affected. They believe this philosophy is only applicable to the weak minded and dependents. Although I understand it, I just don't agree. Some things are better applied theoretically, opposed to actual implementation.

Have you ever heard the phrase, "If it's real it'll come back?"

I've heard that phrase so many times. Do you believe in that? Who decides if it's real? And what does something being real have to do with the relationship being managed properly? People invent all types of adages to make up for their failures and mishaps. That's just an excuse to not put in the necessary work to maintain a relationship. If you're relying on something to come back after you mishandled it, chances are it won't come back. And how eager do you think the person that's been mishandled is to come back to see how much you've changed? Especially after being released from your toxicity and have experienced other people who treated them in the manner they feel as though they needed to be treated. Once someone experiences something new after being accustomed to the same routine for a period of time, it grabs their attention even more. A newly single person is dangerous. Anything could excite them. It could be something simple, but as long as it's different, someone is liable to gravitate towards it. It's a bonus when you're the one garnering their attention, but it makes you sick when you're witnessing it happen at the expense of your mishandling.

Once you start seeing the simple shit that's amusing them, you don't even know if you want them back after that. Or if you could ever look at them the same. Did their interest change, or do they cling on to anything just to feel wanted? I hate when people put up with anything just to say that they have something. Of course, the person who got left would be the one to attempt to define "put up with anything." It's just weird seeing how people move after departure. They begin liking all this new shit that you've never presented to them. It's disgusting. Do people ever start looking unfamiliar during this stage? It doesn't make you look at them in a different light? It's scary. The two of you took a break from each other to reevaluate life and your standing, and you see that they've completely altered into a version of them you never seen before.

Did your partner ever tell you a list of things you should never worry about? Then later on down the line, that list was the exact thing that you had to worry about? It's hard to trust someone who gives a speech of things to never worry about. That list is a list of behaviors or actions that they typically indulge in but mention that you shouldn't be concerned about it just to implement some sort of reverse psychology to deter you from believing the real them isn't the real them. You are the worries you try to prevent.

If you didn't know me, you could possibly assume I'm speaking on a past situation of mine due to how passionate and flustered I often get. If you know me, you know I'm speaking on a past situation of mine due to how passionate and flustered I am. Why is it so hard to delete someone from our memory bank? Is it because you miss them, or because you didn't deserve them in the first place? Same thing, right? I still think it's crazy how she switched up after giving me that speech. But this isn't about me or her. I hate saying us.

Do you think someone can come back from being separated and continue on with the relationship? You believe the transition can be seamless? Me neither. It never really works out that way. You'd be silly to think so. In the rare occasion you were to experience someone returning back to you after the agreed departure, there's no way you can assume they're happier than they were before the break. For entertainment purposes, let's say they do come back happy, restored, and ready to put everything behind and spend their life with you. How would you honestly feel about that? I don't know about you, but that wouldn't sit right with me. I'd think I'm getting played or taken advantage of. I'm not for anyone's convenience. I'm not really with all that realizing you messed up, and you just needed some time to get your life in order bullshit either. We just have to call it for what it is. You thought you could find better, so you agreed with the "break" as an insurance policy; just in case you arrived at the conclusion that you couldn't do better. Or maybe you could, but that "do better" just didn't want you. So, you courted them, they made you look dumb or feel inadequate, and here you are, ready to cash in on my policy. I'm not anyone's insurance policy. Although, I do wonder how much my policy would be worth. We always talk about knowing our worth, it would just be interesting to actually have a direct and concise way of knowing it out. I guess there's really no way to figure that out. But yeah, I'm not with that. You were better off not attempting to come back to the relationship if that was your plan.

Some people are just adept at sensing when they're getting played. It's actually a talent to be able to identify this. You know how many gullible people I see that can't detect ill and deceitful intentions? That couldn't be me. I couldn't be them. Being naïve to someone's bullshit isn't in my nature. You can't perform acts of personal expediency with me. I won't allow it. My heart isn't built for convenience. I'm not hindsight worth. Second chances are a privilege, not a claw to use at the other person's expense when the relationship goes bad.

If they were to come back in good spirits, would you even want them? Especially knowing and realizing they've become happier due to time apart? How can people deal with knowing they're not the place where their partner's happiness derived from? I question all happiness that's created from an outside source. It isn't real if it didn't stem from me; and that's just how I feel about that.

If you were to feel a way about them being happy when they return, that mean you were hoping they'd be distraught, right? Hoping they'd beg for you to understand that the two of you are better together than apart? I love when they beg. I love when people are submissive. I love when they show that they are lost without me. I love when they make it clear that they can't do better than me. I love it when I can notice that they ain't shit without me, without making it obvious. I can just sense it. I love it when I'm the only source their happiness can derive from. Having so much influence in someone's life, that they are willing to put themselves in vulnerable situations and ask for forgiveness is a beautiful feeling. Everyone should experience this at least in their lifetime. And those who are good at garnering this act, knows that most of times, they're the ones that caused the conflicts in the relationship. To be able to be the person at fault and be able to manipulate them enough to have them believe that they're the one who has to apologize, is beautiful.

But all tangents aside, wouldn't that make you question whether you're enough for someone? That they were able to garner and attain what they need from another person? Could you trust them? It has to sit in the back of your mind that if the two of you were to ever hit another rough patch, they'd be liable to go back to whoever installed that happiness in them while the two of you were separated. Because let's be honest, whoever they were entertaining, didn't just disappear when they come back to you. No one just completely leaves someone behind; at least that soon. How realistic is that?

Do you think the person they were entertaining left the picture on their own, or did your partner drop them after they came to their senses? That doesn't even matter honestly. It just wouldn't sit right with me. Maybe it's insecurity issues, or whatever you want to call it; I just know I won't be involved in it. Now you're putting my health and sanity at risk because you decided to magically come to your senses. Just don't let me find out you're back due to someone else's terms. Whatever you do, just don't let me find that out. That's beyond disrespectful. I guess it does matter.

Do you have one hard rule during assigned breaks, or just a bunch of small ones to keep them from finding happiness outside of you? I guess the break wouldn't be as fun if there were rules. My mind is so corrupted and filled with negative ideologies and practices, that I'd think my partner would be doing all the wrong that they could during the break. I mean, because clearly doing good wasn't adventurous enough if we ended up in this situation. I hate having this type of mindset, but this is the same kind of space I thrive and come to most realizations in. What state of mind are you in when you put the most shit together? I feel like it happens most often when the psyche is in an uncomfortable setting. That's when you're most creative. I'd be in my head fully believing that my partner was having sex with the person they been wanting to fuck while they were involved with you. We all got that one person we'd engage with sexually if we weren't already involved with someone. You know if anything were to ever happen, that's the first person you'd hop in bed with. It's almost human instinct to have such backup plans in case certain situations don't pan out. If you're in a relationship and reading this, I'm sorry. Nobody wants to know that their partner has someone in mind that they're willing to indulge with sexually. It'll be hard to ever look at your partner the same if you have the belief that they're liable to do that.

I especially feel bad for the partner of the person reading this because now everything they do is liable to be over analyzed. You'll start looking for signs that aren't present. Everything they do will be taken into consideration. That's not the healthiest of routes, but if that's what has to get done to protect yourself, then by all means take the necessary precautions.

The more I think about it, the crazier that seems to me. Your partner really has another person in mind that they'll sexually entertain while the relationship is active. Has your partner ever initiated an argument with you for what appeared to be for no reason at all? I understand arguing for the purpose of wanting sex from your partner, but that isn't what I'm talking about. You think to yourself what you could've done to cause them to react that way. Have you ever wondered why they randomly bring up old shit that they allegedly forgave you for? They're just planting that seed to do what they really want to do with someone else. And I hate to seem so pessimistic, but somebody has to be it. There's probably a person of interest that recently got in contact with them, which is leading them to create a bullshit atmosphere with. It's all a ploy so that they can indulge without feeling as guilty if they were to just cheat. So, whenever a random argument surfaces, don't even respond; just take mental notes because there's nothing you can do when someone already has their mind made up. At that point, you just have to recognize and accept it for what it is. If they want to fuck around, it's going to happen.

This is exactly why I'm against relationships. You avoid certain dilemmas by extracting yourself from such arrangements. Being responsible for, and with someone else's feelings is serious. Being responsible with your body is serious. That shit is important when it comes to me. That should be the only rule in relationships or assigned breaks; no sex with another person. There's too many ties involved when you share your body with another person. Until there's a way to know for certain that loyalty of the person you like is guaranteed, I don't need to put myself in situations that can potentially damage my sanity.

One of the reasons why I'm so adamant on believing there should be the one strict rule is because once you give yourself away like that to someone else, you've now invited them into our realm. Bad enough we couldn't work out, now you're taking responsibility for someone else's feelings? You can't be irresponsible like that. Imagine being the person that was 'used' as your space filler during the break. You don't think they feel entitled to you in some way? You don't think they're affected by whatever moves you make? Even if that wasn't your intent, you're not in control how someone perceives it. And the fact that they didn't have to do much to garner your attention in the first place, due to inevitable vulnerability after separating from your partner, makes them even more attached and entitled because they mistook your vulnerability for genuine life. That's a dangerous game to play. Nothing is more dangerous than a newly single woman; even if it's temporary. They'll have you believing whatever perception you have is true; not even realizing they're moving cunningly on their own accord.

That's scary. Were you ever unfortunate enough to witness how a man who feels entitled acts? I mean live, right in front of you? It's sad. Its obnoxious. Witnessing a grown man trying to police a woman has to be some sort of mental illness. I don't even want to play around with that; especially in this climate, where everyone is self-diagnosing themselves. That's beyond unhealthy. I don't know if that has become a trend, but it's annoying.

At what point do you just give up on an individual? After having more time to yourself during the break, when do you realize you're better off without sharing the same space with one another. That has to be a frightening thing; realizing you're better off without the person you once thought was your everything. Just imagine regarding someone as your everything, then departing. After experiencing that shit, it makes you not want to ever get involved again.

One more thing and I'll begin this book. Do you think the relationship worked at first because their partner shielded whatever side of them that caused the relationship to be complicated? You were happy, comfortable and securely vulnerable enough to finally give yourself to them. We all shield something; it's a protective mechanism we all employ to guard against anything that could cause us to regress. It seems as though soon as you make yourself vulnerable and comfortable with someone, they switch up on you. They start to pull out those same insecurities and behaviors you initially tried to shield. That's the weirdest shit ever. That's just a tactic insecure people implement to divert the attention away from their flaws and low confidence. It's crazy how they use their insecurities as a way to attack your insecurities. You have to be a sick kind of person to indulge in that type of behavior. So, can you blame someone who opts not to show you all aspects of them because they're aware of how it can be used against them? I know I ask a lot of questions, but work with me. I always ask potential partners, "do you want all of me, or just the parts that benefit the relationship?" And of course, they'll all say that they need all of you, but that's the exact moment when things become complicated. Because honestly, you don't need to be aware of every aspect of them to be happy. Knowledge is power, but it's also a weakness.

My favorite quote; "The key to longevity is to not
know your partner completely". I felt like a genius when I
constructed that. Has there ever been instances when you're
just casually talking, and you utter a great aphorism? You
be feeling a way when the crowd isn't as amazed as you.
You end up repeating it multiple times in your head or
write it in your twitter drafts, just so you can remember it
for another social or intimate setting. We all have those
quotes we feel as though we should be paid for.

But, yeah, it's easy to find the truth in jokes.
Whatever they allow you to show, more than likely, is for
your own good. And once you reach that point to where
one of you feel as though you've exhausted the relationship
to a certain point, walking away could be the remedy.
Everything can't be redeemed. Why are some of us so
against throwing something away? We're well aware that
what we're accepting is cancerous and we still choose to
indulge. We have to work on that. Expect what you accept.

PHASE 2: SMACK THE REMOTE

Often times when I did grab and check the back of the remote, the batteries that my mom tried to preserve weren't in there. But of course, they weren't. We both knew that method was ineffective. So, what was the point? To convince herself that she did all she could before giving up and disposing of them? Is that a thing people do? Exert energy and time into a situation, even if they know things won't change? Isn't that insanity? Doing the same thing over and over again, expecting different results? I guess life wouldn't be as fun if we didn't exhibit this behavior.

I remember I went through this phase where I told myself that I would commit to the gym. We've all been through a phase where we attempted to make going to the gym a habit. And it doesn't matter how badly we need to be there, we always find an excuse to delay going, then get mad at our body for doing what bodies do when it consumes food and doesn't exercise. Honestly, I'm looking at my stomach now as I compose this, and I'm not too comfortable with how it looks. Every time I sit down, rolls start to form on the front and side of my stomach. I hate that. And within 30 minutes of me hating it, I'm eating again.

It's funny because the same things I hate about my body, I love on women. I dislike it when women feel as though they have to reconstruct their body for the sole purpose of fulfilling the idea of an ideal body. If you want to do it because you genuinely want to, then by all means. But to do it to appease a crowd who honestly couldn't care less about you, isn't healthy. I know with social media being a huge influencer, women are prone to believe the women represented on there have the 'perfect body,' when in actuality, their body isn't even their body. Social media attempts to convince you to believe that these types of bodies are the norm and most desired. But who doesn't love a natural woman? Who's turning them down? Don't be confused with the infatuation men seem to have with these modified physiques. Anything that isn't lusted for publicly, is lusted for privately. Remember that.

Whenever I did muster up enough energy to head to the gym, I always found myself doing the bare minimum. I'd work on a machine for a few minutes, then pull my phone out. If I had to guess, I probably logged more minutes on my phone than I did on the workout equipment. I just feel as though the gym is more bearable when you're on your phone. Even though I was doing the bare minimum, I made it a point to at least be there every day. That made me feel better about my poorest efforts. Despite this strategy, you'd think after a few months that there would be some sort of progression, right? No, nothing changed. I still had the same body. I could've ate better as well. I heard that nutrition is just as important as the exercise. But let's be real, attending the gym regularly is a task within itself, so also having to limit and carefully choose what I eat wasn't the best recipe. I guess it's all about commitment. Commitment is a scary word. But I'll get back to that later.

I didn't have the best diet, but still. We're talking about months of consistent, minimal dedication, and seeing no change in results. Even though progression wasn't made in a physical way, my psyche felt good. It was at ease. So therefore, I felt as though if I were to never see results from my minimal efforts, I couldn't blame myself. I was actively there, so, how could I? I tried. Maybe I was doing just enough to not cause regression. Not maybe, I was. That was the goal, to balance out my toxic vices. To balance out the long hours of sitting in the same position for hours, while I watch TV. To balance out the constant consumption of liquor. To balance out the inevitable arguments. To balance out the infidelities. To balance out the lack of communication on my end. To balance out mentally giving up, before deciding to physically leave the relationship. I did just enough. Just enough to stop the problems, but not enough to fix them.

What's more important; stopping the bleeding, or healing the wound? They're both vital, but one has to mean more than the other. When you figure that out, let me know.

While my mom was busy putting close to dead batteries in the freezer, I was the one who smacked the back of the remote to get it to function. I found this method way more effective than her antiquated style. Smacking the remote worked for you as well? It worked damn near every time for me. When it started to die out and cause complications, a simple smack of the remote was all that was needed. I didn't live by my mothers' mantra of, 'they're not dead, they just need a break.' Whenever an issue occurred, it was just in my nature to fix it in a timely manner. I hated waiting to see how it manifested. I had to intervene. Did you ever let things play out, with the hopes of it naturally getting better? Hoping that time fixed a situation rather than effort was not my style. Even even though I didn't agree with putting the batteries in the freezer as an effective method, a freezers job is to literally preserve items. I'm not oblivious to the fact that it makes sense, it just isn't the correct way to handle uncertainty. Have you ever met someone who'd rather hoard something, than to dispose of it because they feel as though it should always be theirs? Even if that something isn't benefiting them at all? They'll opt to shelf it instead of dispose of it. That couldn't be me. I can't shelf my issues; especially in a relationship. I can't just put things on reserve because I'm not sure what to do with them. I can't just hope that seclusion leads to things getting better. I can't do it. I'm a hands-on kind of person. I need to be hands on with things I'm involved in. I need to be in control of how things get handled.

Smacking the remote enables me to address issues in the relationship quicker than if I were to wait it out and use my mothers' technique. The batteries dying, and the remote malfunctioning represents the issues in the relationship. Me smacking the remote against something is me attempting to try and find a quick solution to whatever problem we're enduring, opposed to actually trying to solve the complications at hand by waiting it out. Leaving issues alone is bothersome. And as we all know, when it comes to men, we want instant gratification. We need to see the results of something as soon as we do what we felt as though is the remedy for a solution. We don't have the patience to invest in a project and hope that the results are what we need them to be. But that's just like a man, trying to solve every problem without taking into account of how our woman feels about our method. They want to be handled with care, even if that means delayed solutions for important concerns. I've recently learned that women don't always want a man to assuage the situation; but to understand them, and handle with delicacy.

I could see how someone would say that I'm taking the easy way out of complications by opting to smack the remote. And whoever gives that assumption credence, is correct. But what's wrong with taking the easy way out sometimes? Sometimes, the easy way out is also the smartest way out. People have this belief that is the route taken didn't require a lot of strategy, or tiring work, then it can't be valued as effective as someone who employed methods that require arduous work. Simplicity wins most of the time. Don't you hate when people over complicate a simplicity?

Losing a good woman or man because you over analyzed a situation in the relationship will always haunt you. A relationship ending due to not doing enough, happens all the time. So, to have one end due to you doing too much always intrigues me. Because it's true; because it happens. Then when it's all over, you ponder about it, and question why you did so much, especially when that's not your regular behavior. If it's not genuinely an act you perform, don't try to overcompensate and feel the need to go out of your way to do so. I don't understand that. The person you made yourself out to be in the beginning stages is what garnered their attention; so why switch it up? Once you have them, you have them. Once you alter, you put them in a position to feel as though you've changed, which potentially can lead to departure. Don't be that person that loses someone due to conforming to an identity your partner didn't sign up for.

Although I'm an advocate for the of smacking the remote, I am aware of the faults that come along with applying this method. Sometimes, you have to hear the situation out instead of trying to solve the issues on your own. Everything can't be diagnosed as quick as it's uncovered. If the issue arises that your woman feels as though you don't care about her like you once did, the natural act of most men in their effort to debunk that thought, would be to go out and buy flowers or something of importance. Anything they feel that will satisfy that void she voiced. There will be times when you encounter women who would take the gifts and accept this gesture as a reassurance piece and be content. Some women are shallow like that. Okay, not shallow; but some women will often accept anything they haven't been accustomed to receiving in prior relationships. Those kinds of gestures won't work for most women; especially if they're used to that kind of treatment. It's hard to be impressed with something you're accustomed to or can get on your own. These types of women appreciate effort, not materialistic things. While you're trying to passive aggressively assuage the situation by attempting to finance her happiness, all she really wants you to do is give her attention. To smack her ass while you're playing the game. To joke with her while one of you are cooking. To rub her butt after work. To kiss her forehead in public. All things that don't require anything except effort. You have to appreciate a woman who values simplicity when it's genuine. If she complains that you go out too much, don't smack the remote with your solution being to stay in the house. Although that suggestion could be a remedy for her concerns, that's not what she wants you to do. She still wants you to have fun, but just with her. So instead of opting to stay home, take her out with you. I never understood why men don't voluntarily bring their women to functions with them. You have the most fun with your woman. That's what she's trying to say whether she's aware of that or not. She shouldn't have to voice a concern and also have to provide you with ways to fix the issue. I learned that whenever you encounter a problem, the first solution you arrive to isn't the solution that needs to be implemented.

Maybe smacking the remote isn't as beneficial as I thought. You can't mend problems in relationships quickly and expect things to be fine in the near future. It doesn't work like that. The quicker the fix, the higher the probability is of that happening again. Maybe patience is another key to sustainable and healthy relationships. Instant gratification killed a big part of relationships. Everything can't be microwaved. Baking is a strategy that can be employed as well. Food always tastes better when it's been in the oven. That's the solution; learn to be a baker instead of a quick fixer. I salute anyone who has the patience, and ability, to slowly and delicately handle complications in relationships. That's truly a skill. The more I write, the more I realize that my mother might've been onto something. Even in my own book, that woman still finds a way to outsmart me.

Do you view the batteries dying as some sort of sign? Could you just give up on someone? I don't know about you, but I can't just give up; especially if that wasn't on my agenda. I can't give up on the person I conjured up baby names with. I can't give up on the person I check on every day. I can't give up on the person I told my family about. I can't give up on the person who I believe I can't live without. I can't give up on the person I said I would never leave. And even at its worst, I still can't give up on the person who believes we've ran our course. I just can't. I wasn't molded like that. I don't lose interest fast, I gain it slow. When I get to the point where I consciously choose to indulge, I don't have plans on departing. But who are we to fight what God has planned for us?

Batteries are meant to be replaced, not replenished...

...

Jameel Watson

<u>NOTES</u>

<u>NOTES</u>

PHASE 3: REMEMBER THAT SONG?

Why does it seem like they always become obsessed with you when the relationship is over? That's weird to me. The way you've been telling them how they should've treated you when things weren't going well, is the exact behavior they start to exude. I hate when they appear to have transformed into whom I was praying they would become once the relationship ended. People are fickle like that. You give them multiple warnings on the consequences of their mistreatment of you, but they choose not to take heed to it until you finally commit to leaving. Be cautious; people will purposely drive you to the point of departure, just to stroke their own ego. You don't know how much control and influence you have on someone until you see if you're able to get them back after the point of no return. That takes a certain skill. Some people would opt to lose you, get you back, then treat you right; opposed to treating you right in the first place. It takes a certain amount of discipline and maturity to be done with a situation. And in the same token, it also takes a lack of communication and immaturity to be done with a situation.

Have you ever made an impulsive decision to end a relationship due to how you were feeling at the moment? You don't really think about the lasting impact of that decision, you just want to cut ties with the situation you deemed as toxic and unhealthy. Then days later, even minutes for some people, you start to regret pulling the trigger like that. It's the worst feeling when you have regrets. With some individuals, after making a decision like that, even if they didn't really want to do it, they'll never revisit it and apologize. It's depressing; they'll allow lack of communication on their end, to finalize a relationship that they weren't yet finished with. Just as adamant and timely we are when calling other people out for their bullshit, that same energy has to be mustered up when it comes to our own selves. Don't miss out on the person you want to be with, due to a lack of communication and a lack of self-accountability.

But how do you know who you're supposed to be with? Do you belong with your soulmate, or your life partner?

Your soulmate is a match for you regardless of your current or pending situation. Don't allow things like location, time, and already being involved with someone be an excuse to not be with the person you have the most chemistry with. There's been a few times when someone caught my attention while I was currently involved with someone else. And some of us get those impulses to act on it. And to this day, I can't say that I regret ever risking my relationship. I'm not on earth for a long time, so when certain opportunities I feel are beneficial for me, of course I'll take the chance. You'd be a fool not to. Don't allow your girlfriend or boyfriend to get in the way of your soulmate. I understand the loyalty perspective, but you can't help who you connect with. I hate when people stay loyal to a situation just because they met that individual first; it's not about being there first. It's about who replenishes you to your desired amount after giving energy to your partner. Never feel obligated to remain in a space which you feel you've outgrown.

The first three people that you choose to romantically involve yourself with, are potential soulmates. Once you've passed that threshold, the opportunity to obtain one is gone. Be careful with whom you give your energy to.

How careful are you when it comes to choosing the person you enter into a relationship with? With a soulmate, you don't get a lot of time or opportunity to come across one often. They're rare. If you could locate them anytime throughout your life, the value of them would decrease. I can't augment the value of something if it can be easily obtained. And believe me, this shit isn't easily obtainable. People go their whole life looking for their soulmate, not knowing it's because they should've stopped a long time ago. You can't deal with multiple people and think later on in life you'll find your soulmate. The more people that you've attached yourself to in the quest of finding the "right one", the more you've diluted yourself. The qualities your soulmate is looking for, that you possess, can't be identified as clearly as they should due to your attributes being depleted from giving too much to those who were undeserving. It's a scary world out here; nobody wants to be alone, but nobody wants to involve themselves with individuals who aren't able to reciprocate the same energy and emotion that you emanate.

Do you make your romantic decisions based off a certain moment that amplifies your interest in that person, or do you take into consideration the longevity of involvement between the two of you? I ask because I'm curious. Since my theory states your soulmate is located within the first three people you indulge with, that means you have to be cautious with your decision on who you give yourself to. This is very important to understand. At a younger age, life revolves around want. I want this. I want that. I want to go here. I want, want, want. Rarely do you go for need at the beginning of your adult life. The people you involve yourself with at these early stages are there because you want to involve yourself with them. It's a conscious decision. You search for the exact things you feel as though you deserve. It's a fun process, isn't it? You get to deny those who want your time, due to you not believing that they are worth your effort. What is it about appropriately denying people that spikes your ego? The more people you refuse to give your energy to, the more energy you get. It's a weird feeling. And the best part is that you can afford to waste time because it isn't imperative that you have to commit to longevity. It's a great space. It amuses me how a weird feeling can be captured in such a euphoric atmosphere. But the greater the space, the less you notice the potential downfalls of whoever you're attaching yourself to.

Yes, having the ability and mobility to entertain anyone you want is vital to one's happiness, but if you subscribe to the notion that your soulmate is located within the first three people you're in a relationship with, you also have to be meticulous about the people you choose. You don't want romantic liberation to be the cause for not being able to enjoy your soulmate. We all get caught up with simultaneously giving other people our time because we're so-called free spirits and can do what we want. Don't get caught up in that. Don't be that person who reminisces about old times, rather than enjoying your time with that same person you're reminiscing about.

But then again, maybe people live for telling those stories. Maybe they're a better storyteller than a partner. It happens. The reality is, everyone doesn't want a soulmate. Some actually believe that they don't want or need one to obtain happiness. Whether that perspective is foolish or not, is not up to anyone but that individual to determine. People have to realize that there are other ways to feel alive. Happiness can derive from more than just romantic pairings. Being single does not mean discontentment.

Anyone you choose to romantically involve yourself with after your first three love interests, are life partners candidates.

Your life partner is less adventurous but could be more vital as it pertains to sustainability throughout life. The emotion and chemistry might not reach the heights that a soulmate could take you, but you're better suited for life. You work well together, and the involvement promotes the careers and stability of the two of you. Both people are better together than apart. Isn't that the best; when the two of you are greater together than apart? You're still able to function alone, but it just feels better when you can produce at optimal level. And sometimes, you don't even like one another, but you know that you're unable to manage without one another. Life is harder without one another. I don't know, I find that interesting. You have to appreciate a connection like that. Life finds a way to humble everyone and knock us on our ass, so having stability is something you'll need and want to maintain.

Ten percent of life is what happens to you, ninety percent is how you respond. Life is built for bullshit to happen. None of us are privileged enough to be absolved from the trials and tribulations that come with living. How you recover from such impediments, is what ultimately builds and strengthens character. It doesn't matter how strong we are, we all need help. To have a partner to rely on when your strongest efforts aren't strong enough, is a blessing. Life hates it when you are able to overcome its adversities. Being able to respond with a strong foundation and support is something we all need. This doesn't mean that you are not able to receive this from your soulmate, but most often, soulmates are more of an emotional bond, opposed to logical.

Honestly, reading over that last passage, that shit just sounds boring. Stability is boring. A strong foundation is boring. Relying on someone is boring. I can't live like that. I don't know; maybe I have this perspective because I'm still young, and slowly beginning to exit the soulmate stage of my life. I can't really relate to the adjustments that come with being involved with a life partner. I mean, I can but I can't. I don't want to. I feel as though I jeopardize my writing every time I enable my viewpoints to be clear. I hate interrupting myself.

Do you appreciate security over unconditional desire? After you've had your fun, you realize that there's a new side of life you need to adapt to. The real world is scary after you've had your fun. Security has to be one of the most vital things you wish to have in adult life. You want to have that big home. You want to be able to travel without worrying if you can pay future bills. You want to be financially stable so that you can support more than just yourself. You want to have a partner that you can rely on when you're unable to support more than just yourself. You have to value security. But you also have to realize that the person that can enable all this to occur, isn't always the person you're meant to be with.

Have you ever been in a healthy relationship, but occasionally have flashbacks of previous ones that weren't as beneficial and healthy as the one you're currently in? You enjoyed the uncertainty in the past relationships over the one that's treating you better. It happens all the time. It's scary knowing that sometimes you have to adapt and accept a life that doesn't promote your full happiness, just so that you can live a life that allows you to live comfortably. I don't know whether to appreciate it, or frown upon it. That's what makes this interesting. You have to make a decision on when to become involved, and then decide what you prioritize. But I guess there's worse scenarios you could be involved in. You could be happy with your partner, with no direction in life. You could be happy with your partner, and unable to accomplish the things you want to, due to inability to depart and secure your wants that are beyond the relationship. Deciding which conundrum to embrace is so dope to me.

But why can't someone have the best of both worlds? Why can't you find the person you're meant to be with and have security that enables the both of you to live comfortably? Mainly because life doesn't work that way. A friend of mine responded to this thought by saying it is attainable, because her God says it is. Which is cute; it's understandable. I'm all for God's path and power, but some things are better off in theory, rather than applied to real life. Everyone would have who and what they wanted if we abided by getting the best of both worlds. That would simplify life. Life isn't simple, at all. We wouldn't have ex's. We wouldn't have stories. We wouldn't have the emotional scars that we look forward to our woman or man to heal. We wouldn't have a reason to fight for what we have. We wouldn't have growth. Growth has always been an interesting term to me; mostly because I don't believe in it. Never did. It didn't make sense to me. I think people unravel, not grow. But that's neither here nor there. The point is, we wouldn't have these things that ultimately create our character, if it wasn't for the journey of not getting what we desired.

Why does it seem like you arrive to the most realizations when the relationship is over? It feels like everything comes to you; the questions, where everything went wrong. It hits you all at once. Everything becomes clear. But of course, everyone can see better when the blindfold is unveiled. What if I told you that departure is the best part of a relationship? Have you ever realized that whenever you exit a relationship, you often learn more about yourself? You get a new understanding of who you are and what you deserve. I love that part. I love finding out who I really am. I love being aware of what I deserve. And oddly, I love that it took for the relationship to end for me to reminisce and come to these conclusions. I love reminiscing.

Have you ever been listening to music and then a throwback song that you forgot that you loved comes on? You start to think back to how you felt in the moment when the song first premiered. You start bobbing your head to a beat you haven't heard in years. And then you're stuck. There's nothing like getting trapped in nostalgia for 4 minutes. You remember how you felt at the time. You remember what you were going through at that time. You remember how good that song made you feel at the time. You remember the whole climate. It's just a feeling you get that makes you appreciate the song even more due to the connections you made with it. Then when the song ends, you start to come down from your high because you recognize the times that you're currently in, is nothing like how it was back then. And that's why we love throwbacks. You understand you can never get that moment back, but you can appreciate it for what it was and what it meant to you at that time.

Why don't we treat the ending of relationships in the same manner? Why can't we accept what is? I hate seeing people try to get an expired moment back. That isn't healthy for either party. You appreciate the throwback because you don't hear it often. You appreciate it because it enables you to temporarily escape. You appreciate it because it impacted your life at some point in time. You appreciate it because you can't get that time back. Once you keep attempting to regain that feeling, it no longer becomes a feeling. It loses its importance. You recognize that it was better off as a memory than something constant. But then again, I get it. Once you hear a song that made you feel a certain way, it's difficult to move on from it. Once someone makes you feel a certain way, it's difficult to just leave them as a memory. Songs become classics due to their relevance and joyous aura they give off. When you like a song that someone else dislikes, and they question why you like it; you can't really explain it to them. I never knew music and relationships correlated so much.

What everyone else might deem as toxic, only you and that person can really define it, which can make that bond seem stronger than what it's supposed to be. I used to hate when people outside my relationship advised me to depart from someone because it was hard for them to notice the good in them. I see the good in them. Why are you telling me what I should accept? And most importantly, why is this speech, more often than not, delivered from someone who is in a worse predicament than you? The audacity of some people. But I guess that makes me a hypocrite to speak like that. Honestly, it doesn't matter who else can see the good in the people I deal with. Only I need to see it.

Think about why your last relationship ended. I love hearing people's reasoning, because for the most part, it never involves them being the blame. It's always the other person. Rarely do you come across people who own up and take accountability for their role in the downfall of a relationship. It might seem weird, but I think whoever takes the stance of accepting accountability for the demise, in a way, are admitting that they weren't really invested in the relationship. If you are aware that you are the one causing complications, why not cease that behavior? You know that if you act a certain way, then there's an outcome that comes with it. If you are aware of the outcome, why continue to do it? Why put yourself in a situation where you have to apologize and be the catalyst to your partner's regression? I've never seen the worth in that.

But then again, the things I thought I found worth in, never worked out for me. I hate when it seems like I get personal too much. I've put a lot of time and stock into my previous partners, just for them to shit on me. Just for them to turn their backs on me. For them to forget that I was there for them when no one else was. To ultimately switch up on me when I showed the vulnerability that they asked for. It's almost as if once you get to the point of caring, the relationship ends. All of my dealings ended when I started to care. Now I see why people choose not to change in relationships. I swear everything makes more sense when the relationship ends. Remain the same person that first attracted them.

And what is it about treating people like shit that causes them to be more attached to you? I need to know the reasoning behind that. Is their goal to attempt to change you, or is just some weird liking they've acquired? The less I cared, the more controlled they relinquished to me. I'll come back to that. – come back to it in final stage

Be aware that you can't handle everyone like that. That's the reason why I'm here writing this. I'm sorry I handled you like that. You didn't deserve that. You did nothing besides be a good woman to me. But why? I didn't ask you to be one. Yes, I required it, but I didn't ask for it. What were you doing trying to save me? I hate when people go out of their way to do shit I didn't ask for. All you had to do was... I don't know, actually. I just wish you didn't do that. I wish you didn't put me in situations that forced me to be a better man. I wish you didn't make me want to learn more. I wish you were mature enough to deal with my bullshit. I wish you didn't offer so much. I wish you weren't as smart as you are. Then maybe you wouldn't have realized that your worth was more important than the situations I put you through. I hate that I keep encountering intelligent women. I'm sorry you're reading this, and I wasn't man enough to say it in person. 1.4.3

Do you believe it's possible for a relationship to fail because your partner offered too much? Do you think that's a valid reason? Would you accept that response if it was told to you? It seemed as though the more my partner offered, the more intimidated I became. It's a feeling of knowing that you have to produce and match what they're providing, or else you'll get labeled as inadequate. Nobody wants to be labeled as that. Even if your partner doesn't say it, you being aware is what hurts the most. That always hurts; knowing something negative about your character without it being said to you, yet the characteristic is felt by others. I hated feeling inadequate. I hated knowing the person I was dealing with was too good for me. I hated knowing that it didn't matter what I brought to the table, anyone could bring what I brought. And that made me feel some kind of way about myself.

Have you ever been in relationships where you were completely aware that your partner didn't offer as much as you? How did you handle that? I don't know about you, but that made me become more interested. I felt as though I could do whatever I wanted. Why do you feel as though you can go out and find better? You can't find better if I'm your person you're currently involved with. But, I was never one of those people to voice it, I just moved in that manner. I was arrogant with my body language, mannerism and presence. And in a weird way, I still felt like I was the one that needed to thank them. After all, they were the ones responsible for my egotistical ways.

Due to their acceptance of me, I stuck around longer. I felt like that was the agreement; I stick around and give you everything you need, as long as you accept my behavior. I'm not sure how even of an exchange that was, but it worked until it stopped working. It made me feel wanted. It made me feel needed. It made me more decisive with my decision making. It made me feel comfortable.

I committed more to people who didn't offer as much as me but shied away from those who did. The more I write, the more I understand why I ended up in one failed relationship after another. Who am I to say whether what someone is offering is good enough or not? Who gave me the authority to determine that? But also, who am I to not be particular about what I choose to deal with? I have the responsibility and ability to make sure I deal with what I want to deal with. People have it fucked up by thinking that you're not allowed to set standards for yourself. If you don't want to deal with someone because you feel as though they're lacking something, so be it. Your excuse can be as dense as you want it to be. You don't need to exercise euphemisms.

But it's weird to me how people who had a lot to offer scared me away. Or rather made me hesitant. They made me second guess if I should indulge or not. I wasn't used to people who could carry responsibility like me. I wasn't used to dealing with people who would be completely fine without me. I wasn't used to people making me live up to all the false hope that I had sold to others. I was used to dealing with people who offered considerably less than me and making shit work from their brokenness.

I've spent about four days trying to think of a transition for my next passage, and for some reason it just isn't coming to me. And honestly, I hate smooth transitions. People don't really think like that. Naturally, thoughts are scattered. Nobody thinks in a perfect line. Everything doesn't have to be perfect. I get jealous and irritated when I read literature that seems to flow too well.

Where's the human element? How are all of your thoughts able to consistently be cohesive? But I guess whatever works for you, works for you. So, here's me, transitioning into the next passage.

I love buffets. I find myself going there more often than I should. Who can turn down all of that food for their advertised price? Every time I enter and head to the food section, I have a habit of standing there for minutes trying to decide what to get. You would think that since there's so many choices, making a decision shouldn't be complicated. I thought the same thing. The more options I saw, the more hesitant I was to commit to a choice. I was thinking that maybe I should just put everything on my plate, and whatever I finished, is what I finished. More often than not, I never finished. I was there stuffed, with a bunch of food on my plate. I always felt as though me not finishing my food meant that I wasted money. I just felt obligated to do so. But after not being able to consume it all, you think to yourself how you would've been completely satisfied if you had just gotten less. We think just because a lot is offered, we're obligated to have access to all of it.

Don't you hate greedy people? Just because you have access to it, doesn't mean you should utilize it and abuse it. That's how things become spoiled. When you go grocery shopping, do you purchase by bulk, or buy what you need? That's how items go bad; obtaining something you don't need but want because you have the ability to get it. It seems like everything makes sense when you add food to the situation. But now I get it. The more options the buffet gave me, the longer it took me to get comfortable. It works the same way with relationships. It's scary when they offer too much. When they offer too much, you're not even sure of what you need anymore. That self-doubt starts to creep up and worry you. And in a relationship, people don't have the time for you to be indecisive. I learned that the hard way.

Whenever I go to a convenient store in my neighborhood to buy hot food, it's a different story. I always seem to be decisive with my choices. For the most part, the only hot food options are burgers, chicken tenders, hoagies and cheesesteaks; with a bunch of variations within those options. And every time I go in there, I know exactly what I want. And sometimes, the person that's cooking your food, if you go there enough, will already know your order as well. But why is that? Why am I so conclusive with the minimal options that are being afforded to me? You'd think since the selections are limited, it would take me longer to choose. But it didn't. The less that was offered, the easier it was for me to commit to a decision. The less that was offered, the more comfortable I became. The less that was offered, the more control I gained. That's why when I encounter people who don't provide as much as me, I'm willing to commit more to them, than to someone who had the full package.

I understand how some people would think intimidation would play a role in people consciously deciding to disengage and refrain from dealing with someone who has the full package. It makes sense to conclude that. But why do people surmise that the full package is the best package? There is a such thing as being satisfied with less. There's been plenty of instances where I was content with finishing half of my dinner and felt satisfied at the end. It was just enough to do its job. Enough to make me feel comfortable. So, no, it's not intimidation, it's being aware enough to know what's for you.

No One Deserves A Relationship

.   .

The full package - *any attributes from the preferred sex or gender that intimidates you because it puts pressure on you to become a better person. People either succumb to the pressure or embrace it.*

As stated, you learn a lot when the relationship ends. I don't know why people don't embrace this stage more often. Why is it depicted as some sort of stain on your record? People who are always indulging in situations that do not last long, are always, or more often than not, viewed as the cancer or reasoning for things not working out. Sometimes, shit just doesn't work out. That's just the way it is. There isn't always a culprit in these kinds of situations. I always preach to those around me that seem to involve themselves in one failed relationship after another, that you have to know why you're entering the relationship in the first place. Sadly, some people just want to be able say they have somebody. The older you get, you learn that entering a relationship for the sole purpose of not being lonely isn't healthy. When you begin to espouse that type of philosophy, you'll always feel as though you have to attach yourself to someone else to feel complete, alive and accepted.

In a weird way, I understand it to a degree. People die in isolation. It works the same way with jail and prison. When they put people in confinement as a punishment, it's for them to lose their sanity. It's for them to feel detached from their environment. You lose yourself when you're alone for too long. I'm not one that cares for studies that aren't conducted by me, but I'm sure there's some sort of statistics out there that aligns with my notions. But nobody wants to find themselves in a situation that could promote regression in their psyche.

There are people whom are scared to be by themselves for an extended period of time to avoid finding out who they truly are. You don't really have to define yourself when you're amongst a group or community. Sometimes your environment takes the role of your identity. And don't get me wrong, there's nothing awry about not knowing yourself, because truth is, for the most part, none of us do. We're always learning and getting better, so we'll never truly know ourselves. But as long as you're comfortable in not knowing, you're fine. Awareness is more vital than identification.

Knowing who you are, without any type of attachments or responsibility of others, is vital. You need to unveil that person. You need to unveil the reason that you're here.

Again, know why you're entering the relationship in the first place. Are you looking for longevity, or experience? I don't think that question is thought about when we decide to indulge with people. We just react. We see a face, notice familiarities, get a glimpse of their personality and automatically want to connect ourselves to that person. Then whatever comes from that engagement, is what comes from it. We can't make these decisions on whether we want longevity or experience amid relationship. We all know how difficult it is to think clearly once feelings and history get involved. Don't confine yourself to a situation due to the inability to articulate and determine what your wants and desires are. Once you're in a predicament where you're looking for reasons to stay and reasons to leave, the relationship is already ruined. There's nothing worse than your mind leaving the relationship before your body.

And always remember - Do not make questioning your position in someone's life a habit.

Jameel Watson

PHASE 3: MIND-BODY-SOUL

Mind, Body and Soul are three different people. Typically, those three aspects are what people hope their partner can feed. In my dealings, I don't believe I was ever fortunate enough to have all three fed by one person. And at the same time, I don't believe I ever put myself in a position to offer that to anyone. It seems as though it requires too much energy; energy that I wasn't comfortable exerting. And even still, I couldn't imagine being able to fulfill all three, or come across someone who could.

You never wondered why that was so difficult to obtain? Well, at least from one person, right? Some people opt to deal with multiple partners because in their head, if they can have everything catered to, even if it means it's deriving from multiple people, then they'll take it. We all would. We all have. Have you ever dealt with multiple candidates and thought that you would have the perfect person if you were able to combine all of their attributes? That's the best; when you're dealing with multiple individuals that caters to all of your needs. I would imagine that it's better if one person could, but I've never experienced that. I don't know what that would look like, or how it would feel. I can just assume it's something that we'd all cherish and appreciate.

Personally, I don't think that one person can attend to all three of the main needs. It's impossible; yet it takes a special individual to be able to successfully fulfill two of the three. We've all had that person we would've deemed as perfect if they just had one or two more things to offer. They're always lacking some vital component that makes you feel complete. Why can't life just give us what we want? Why does it seem like everything comes with some sort of conundrum?

Once you realize that only two of the three elements can only be fulfilled by one person, it's on you to prioritize what's important. Often times when we are unable to figure out what we want from potential partners, it's because we're being greedy in our quest. I love being part of the reason. Do you even need to have your mind, body and soul catered to by someone? If they are unable to fulfill one of those, you can't handle the rest? It's all or nothing? Even though I haven't depicted the best portrayal of myself, I'm never dismissing someone who shows up to the table offering two thirds of what's deemed as needed to feel complete. I've entertained people who offered less. I'm able to do that because I feel complete within myself. You shouldn't rely on anyone, or anything for you to feel whole.

If you got everything you wanted, what would you do with it? Where do your values lie when you're unable to get everything you want? What goes into your thought process of deciphering needs? Are you greedy to the point where you'd mess up a potential connection with someone by trying to obtain all three aspects when they've successfully fulfilled two already? Don't be that person that ruins a good situation by forcing something that isn't willingly given or offered. If they could've and wanted to present something to you, they would do so without the pressure of being forced. Once you determine what's important to you, the easier this process becomes.

Jameel Watson

MIND

The mind is fragile, impressionable and delicate. It's one of those things that can make or break you, depending on how it's maintained. It's the only thing that doesn't rest, so you have to be careful with who you give the power to alter it; once it's altered, it's no longer completely yours. Involving yourself with an individual, allows them to influence both; how you think and how you maneuver. Depending on how comfortable you are in your current involvement, this could be a beautiful thing, or a detriment.

The same reasons you praise it, are the same reasons why you despise it at times. It acts beyond your wants. Have you ever noticed how someone's conversation could make you like them more than you normally would if they didn't offer that? We've all been there; liking someone who doesn't meet the criteria of our physical liking but remain intrigued due to their substance. I wonder what kind of chemical releases in the body when you begin to like someone for their conversation. There has to be some sort of term for that. Once you're captured by their conversation, it seems as though you begin to heighten your liking for more of their attributes. They start to look better. They begin to seem funnier. Everything about them augments, all because your mind was being fed. Sometimes all you have to do is feed their psyche to get them to unveil their true selves. The reason why the real them comes out once this euphoric feeling comes about, is because our minds naturally rejects anything we aren't accustomed to. It's always enlightening to see what you uncover about yourself when your mind rejects routine behavior.

And who doesn't want their psyche to be catered to? We all yearn for that. Even though we've repeatedly heard the adage of words not meaning much if actions aren't involved, it's still good to hear it. It's always good to hear it. Reassurance is a big thing in relationships. Even if you know your partner loves, admires and appreciates you, it's a different type of feeling when it's voiced. It takes you to a place of security. It doesn't matter how much you show your partner, being able to articulate your appreciation goes a long way. You can be doing well in school, but the sound of your parents telling you that they're proud can add more feeling. The mind is sensitive, so it's important to treat it as such.

To those that don't care too much for words aligning with action, I completely understand that as well. I was never one to oblige by that mantra. Because honestly, I don't want my words to match my actions. I want my actions to match my feelings. That's the goal. Once that is aligned, the more comfortable I am.

We also want our partners to know what to say when things aren't going well. I've seen many relationships end prematurely due to the right words not being spoken. Even if it wasn't intentional, it's how it's perceived. And the right words have to be said at the right time as well. Timing is just as important as your words; maybe even more. Small complications get exacerbated when we are unable to produce the conversation that needs to be held. And when you are unable to heal a situation, you can never look at that person the same again. It doesn't matter how much you try to uphold the same image of that person, your mind won't allow you to do so.

I hate when I can't look at someone the same whenever a situation arises that puts them at fault. I really do. Holding on to grudges and extracting people out of my life has been something I've tried to refrain from doing. I try to forget. I try to forgive. I try to paint a new picture of those who I believe did a disservice to me. I try to reject the thought that pop up when I see them or if their name is mentioned. But it never really works. Once someone puts you in a position to question their genuineness and motives, you can't look at them the same. Regardless of what your feelings are, the mind won't enable it.

This might seem insignificant, but don't you love it when you're also able to take your partner out in public, and they're well versed with vocabulary? They're able to have abstract and concrete conversations with peers, strangers and potential business associates. That just turns you on in a way. Something so simple as having an eclectic vernacular can cause for your partner to feel a different way about you. Even though, as a grown being, you should have a strong vocabulary. That should just develop with your maturation process. But nevertheless, to have one, is to be appreciated. Most believe your partner is a reflection of you, so when they're able to conduct themselves in a mature manner, it's a bonus.

Jameel Watson

BODY

My personal favorite; mainly because the body is
the only thing you have control of. I'm big on control. And
when it comes to the body, I'm sure everyone else is as
well. You are able to control who has access and who
doesn't. This might sound cheesy, but has someone you
were attracted to ever touch you in a way that caused you to
have goosebumps? The slight shiver will always do
something to you. I miss getting goosebumps. I miss
having someone to give me goosebumps. I feel bad for
people who never experienced that; mainly the men. Why
do men think they're too masculine to enjoy a pleasant
feeling that derives from their woman? As a man, I like
being touched by my woman. I like my head being held or
rubbed when I'm lying on her stomach. How are you
unable to allow yourself to be vulnerable around the
woman that you're entertaining?

Is that a comfortability thing? For certain people
you display certain actions and emotions; I get it. Once we
come to the point of being involved with each other, why
shield yourself from offering everything you have? If I'm
dealing with you, I no longer have to be selective in what I
give you. It takes a lot for someone to get my attention in
the first place, so once I'm with you, I'm ready to give you
my all. I might have to retract that; I don't know. I'll think
about it later.

Intimacy is vital. Even though I believe sex is 90% mental and 10% physical, that latter percentage holds weight. A lot of weight, actually. Whenever I ask people to list off the most important things in a relationship, communication and personality always seemed to be the predominant answers. Then I follow up and ask if they would stay with their partner if they were receiving everything they wanted, but the sexual chemistry was off balanced. And of course, for the majority, the answer was no. So, is it important, or not? Quiet as kept, a lot of relationships have ended due to bad sexual chemistry. Of course, no one would openly admit that to someone they care about, so they take another route to give reason for their departure. I used to think that it was unfortunate that these types of things occurred, but the more I thought about it, I realized that you shouldn't deal with someone who doesn't take care of you sexually.

Who wants to deal with someone who doesn't make them feel comfortable, or wanted sexually? That's supposed to be a place of vulnerable comfort. Yes, I'm letting my guard down as I'm giving you my body, but I want to be comfortable when doing so. I want to be vulnerable enough to be able to share my body. I want to be vulnerable enough to share that space with you. I want to be comfortable enough to want to be vulnerable. I want to feel comfortable enough that you won't abuse that space we share. Vulnerability and comfortability goes hand in hand. It always has and will.

But besides that, we all want our bodies to be catered to. We want to be comfortable when in the presence of each other. I feel as though physical comfort is underrated.

As much as I despise the modern-day usage of "vibes", it's relaxing when you can allow an aura to momentarily take the place of verbal communication. It's dope when your body does the talking for you. I want to be at ease when I'm around you. I want to be relaxed when I'm lying next to you. I want to feel restful when you touch me. I want to feel uneasy when someone who isn't you touches me. I hate that feeling of discomfort when someone attempts to break the touch barrier with you. It makes you cringe. It could be the exact place that I like my partner touching, but if it isn't them, it's disturbing. It's always disturbing when it isn't them.

I'm an ears and shoulder kind of person. There's something about those areas that calms me. I don't know, anything above the waist for some odd reason soothes me. It's almost like, the further you are from my private areas, the more intimate the touch is. But we all have those uncommon places that brings about pleasure when our partner touches us. I don't know, I think that's decent.

But the body is more than just how I am with you. When I'm around others, I want the comfort I feel with you to be unattainable; because it is unattainable. It's just a different feeling when that person is yours. When your woman asks you to hold her hand in public, it's not just to look cute, it's because they feel safe and desired. A feeling all women want. Something so simple could mean so much. I used to hate holding hands in public, until I realized it's not for my enjoyment, but my partners'. And my enjoyment then derived from seeing how happy they were.

Jameel Watson

SOUL

Can it be felt without being seen? It's amazing how someone can have an impact on you without being present. Have you ever thought about someone and instantly got in a better mood? That's the best, isn't it? It doesn't even have to be a direct thought, it could be something such as a sound or sight that reminds you of someone. I miss having someone worth thinking about. That shit used to turn my whole day around if it wasn't going well. That's how you know you're in too deep, when the thought of someone has the ability to alter your whole mood. When I think about the person I'm with, that's what I want to happen. Why am I with you if this can't be accomplished? I'm supposed to only be able to enjoy you if you're present? If that's how it has to be, I don't want it. Nobody should want that. Imagine only being able to make your partner feel good when you're around. That's when you find out how strong the bond is, when neither of you can feel one another.

Long distance relationships will tell it all. I've seen people fall under the pressure of not being able to touch their partner. It's almost as if they're not around, they don't exist. That's a scary world. When people succumb to that pressure, they use distance as a way to justify any sort of infidelity. They claim that they needed to fill a void. If the spirit is being nourished how it's supposed to be, there wouldn't be a void. Voids are a product of someone being irresponsible with their feelings; or lack thereof.

Has anyone ever blamed distance, and or lack of something as their reasoning for committing unacceptable acts in the relationship? That's the weakest shit ever. Temptation is never that deep. I'm not risking my relationship for anything that I can get at any time. You should never attempt to risk everything that matters, just for a temporary craving of someone else. Once that craving is satisfied, then what? Your partner finding out is not worth the enjoyment of that moment. Or maybe it was; I'm not the person to determine that. I just know a healthy relationship beats meaningless engagements any day.

The more I write, the more I condemn myself.

It's kind of scary when you think about it. Imagine having that much of an influence over someone. Would you even want to have someone have that much effect over you? That's a lot of responsibility. It's almost dangerous because whatever you do has the capability of affecting your partner, whether negatively or positively.

Do you see why longevity is so hard to obtain? Not to sound like the asshole I actually am, but it's damn near impossible for one person to be able to fulfill all those needs. The mind, body and soul needs to constantly be fed, whether directly or indirectly. To ask or expect someone to tend to all three, is asking them to be disingenuous. That's the only way this can be done; if someone makes it an objective, instead of it happening naturally. If I'm dealing with someone that goes out of their way to attempt to satisfy me, I'm not sure if I'll accept that. Of course, for face value, you would appreciate someone acquiescing to your needs, but it starts to creep in your mind that it isn't genuine. And I don't know about you, but I'm not accepting that. Anyone that that makes it an objective to go out of their way to please you, in my eyes, has alternative motives.

Jameel Watson

<u>NOTES</u>

<u>NOTES</u>

PHASE 4: MAYBE YOU WERE NEVER IN A RELATIONSHIP TO BEGIN WITH

Why do people think they're in a relationship just because they spend more time with each other than apart? As if being together all the time gives credence that there's a relationship in progress. All that really means is that you spend more time with each other, than apart. That's all. People love giving something a name so that they can be comfortable. So they can feel attached. So that they can have something to reference to whenever someone questions it. But giving something a name doesn't mean it exists. It just means it has a name.

Seeing someone's face more often than you see your own means nothing. Sharing the same laughs and taste in music means nothing. Having those late-night drives and long talks means nothing. Sharing the same bed every night means nothing. Waking up to the same face every day means nothing. Taking trips and documenting the moment means nothing. Confessing vulnerabilities and aspiration to one another means nothing. Temporary moments for temporary feelings. Saying "I love You" means nothing. It all means nothing. There's no obligations in relationships. And when there's no obligations, people tend to carry themselves carelessly and commit acts that only benefit themselves, even though they're supposedly responsible for someone else's feelings. Of course, there's an unwritten handbook that people are supposed to abide by, but nothing is official. It's not as if you can pull it out and discuss the details and broken agreements when things go wrong. There isn't anything that protects you from disappointments and abandonment. The more that reality settles within me, the less I'm willing to put myself in such scenarios.

The scariest thing about relationships, is that you can pack up and leave at any moment. Whether you're feeling overwhelmed, underappreciated, or just bored; one can go their separate ways without any repercussions. That's scary; investing so much into someone that could potentially walk away from you at any time. That just screams paranoia. It makes sense why people are hesitant to give their all when dealing with someone; especially nowadays. Who wants to make themselves vulnerable like that? It doesn't matter how much you think you know someone, you'll never know with certainty what's going on in their head. To be that confident in your confidant, that you're willing to repeatedly take the risk of dealing with relationship agony, is a special skill. A naive skill. A gullible skill. One of the rare skills that people shouldn't want to master or obtain. But if a relationship means more to you than your sanity, by all means, indulge.

Isn't it crazy how you can do almost everything with someone, then eventually become strangers again? That's a weird position to be in. You randomly have flashbacks of how happy you were with them. Then you run a timeline of all the highlights and low points of the relationship. You think about how some arguments and disagreements actually weren't as big as the two of you made them out to be at the time. Realizing they could've been avoided if the communication was better. Imagine never talking to someone you thought you'd spend the rest of your life with. It's easy to imagine because most of us have done it. We've all told previous partners lies we knew we couldn't keep. In the moment, you just feel as though you can say anything regarding longevity and love, and it'll sound and feel right. It's supposed to sound and feel right. Sharing intimate sentiments is dope to me. To be able to repeatedly conjure up acts and sayings that display your love and affection is priceless. And then it happens. You go from not spending a day apart from one another, to becoming strangers. I don't know how people do it. Strangers? All the memories you collaborated on? All assurances you gave one another? It just puts you in a different space. An unwanted space. A space that you never want to enter again due to the uncertainty that people provide in relationships.

Every relationship I ever experienced, damaged me. Whether the relationship involved my father or people of interest; they all damaged me. I wasn't the same person I was prior to engaging. I didn't trust the same prior to engaging. My tolerance for bullshit wasn't the same prior to engaging. Everything changed. Everything diminished; whether it be what I offered, or what I allowed. It was probably because I had expectations. Expectations to be cared for. Expectations to have someone to lean one when I'm not strong enough to stand on my own. Expectations to be handled with delicacy. Expectations that they were nothing like the last person I dated. Although, in most occasions, they were exactly like the last person I dated; if not worse. I hate when people say they'll never do me like the people in my past did me, just to turn around and do exactly what the people in my past did to me. How can you hear all the hurt and disappointment I've dealt with, just to put me in the same situations? How are you bold enough to do that? I don't know... Relationships just don't sit right with me. No one deserves them. No deserves the agony that derives from them. No one deserves to involve themselves with someone that promotes toxicity and uncertainty. No one deserves to be responsible for someone else's feelings.

I placed a certain responsibility on others so that the burden I carried wouldn't become a burden to me. Am I wrong for doing that? I should be able to rely on you. If the people you share relationships with are unable to lessen your responsibilities, what are they there for? If we're an item, regardless of the capacity, I shouldn't have to carry the workload as if I'm alone.

Do I appreciate the person that stops the bleeding more than someone who attempts to fix the wound? I don't know. The way people maneuver now, is that, if they do something for you, they feel as though you owe them. They feel entitled. They might not openly say it, but they'll interact with you knowing they did you a favor. They'll be more assertive or more intimate because believe that you're more comfortable or less likely to rebel against they're present due to what they did for you. I hate when people do that. Why does every good act have to come with stipulations? I don't want to be in debt with someone just because they found me at a point in my life where I wasn't myself. People just aren't genuine anymore. So, I don't know. I can't place too much value in someone who stops the bleeding. It's scary because their act of kindness could be genuine. But in this climate, it's all about protecting yourself.

At first, I thought someone attempting to fix my wound meant a lot. I assumed they cared. I assumed they were willing to pause their life to attend to my issues. That takes a different type of dedication to sit there with someone and work something out. Attention to detail and commitment are the biggest attributes you notice during this time. But the more I thought about it, the more cautious I became of someone attempting to patch me up. What's their true purpose for doing so? Why are they taking care of me as if I mean something to them? Don't you hate it when people overthink something? To attempt to fix my wound, means that we're stationary for a long time. I have no choice but to casually get along with you. The danger is when you get comfortable. You might begin the appreciate the act more than the person. That's an uncompromising position. I don't want to be one of those people that mistakes time spent, with likeness. If you spend a good amount of time with someone, naturally, some similarities and interest will begin to align. I fell victim to that on too many occasions. So, I don't know. I'm not sure if I can't trust that person either.

You can't rely on other people to fix your problems. You can't rely on people to heal whatever affliction you have. You don't want to put yourself in a situation where someone could say that they're responsible for anything you've accomplished or healed from. Take accountability for everything that involves yourself. No one can rehabilitate you better than yourself.

NOTES

<u>NOTES</u>

Contact the Author

Email: Jameelwatson215@gmail.com

Twitter: @Meel_Forever

Instagram: Meel_Forever

In addition, if you have any questions, comments, or concerns, use the hashtag #No1Deserves to engage with the author. Thank you.

Contact the Editor

Serena Haeuser: carefoundationphl@gmail.com

Instagram: __Serena1 - Twitter: Serenahaeuser

Made in the USA
Middletown, DE
07 September 2019